The 9 Colours

of 

Vibrant Women

Decode Your Traits and Foster Situation led Self-Leadership !!

The 9 Colours
of
Vibrant Women

Decode Your Traits and Foster Situation led

Self-Leadership !!

RAMYA R. MOORTHY

EKA PUBLISHERS

#118 Ushodaya Enclave, PO Miyapur

Hyderabad 500049 (India)

ekapresshyderabad@gmail.com

www.ekapress.org

First Published in India by Eka Publishers in May 2020

ISBN: 978-81-944712-8-8
FICTION

Printed and bound in India by Eka Publishers

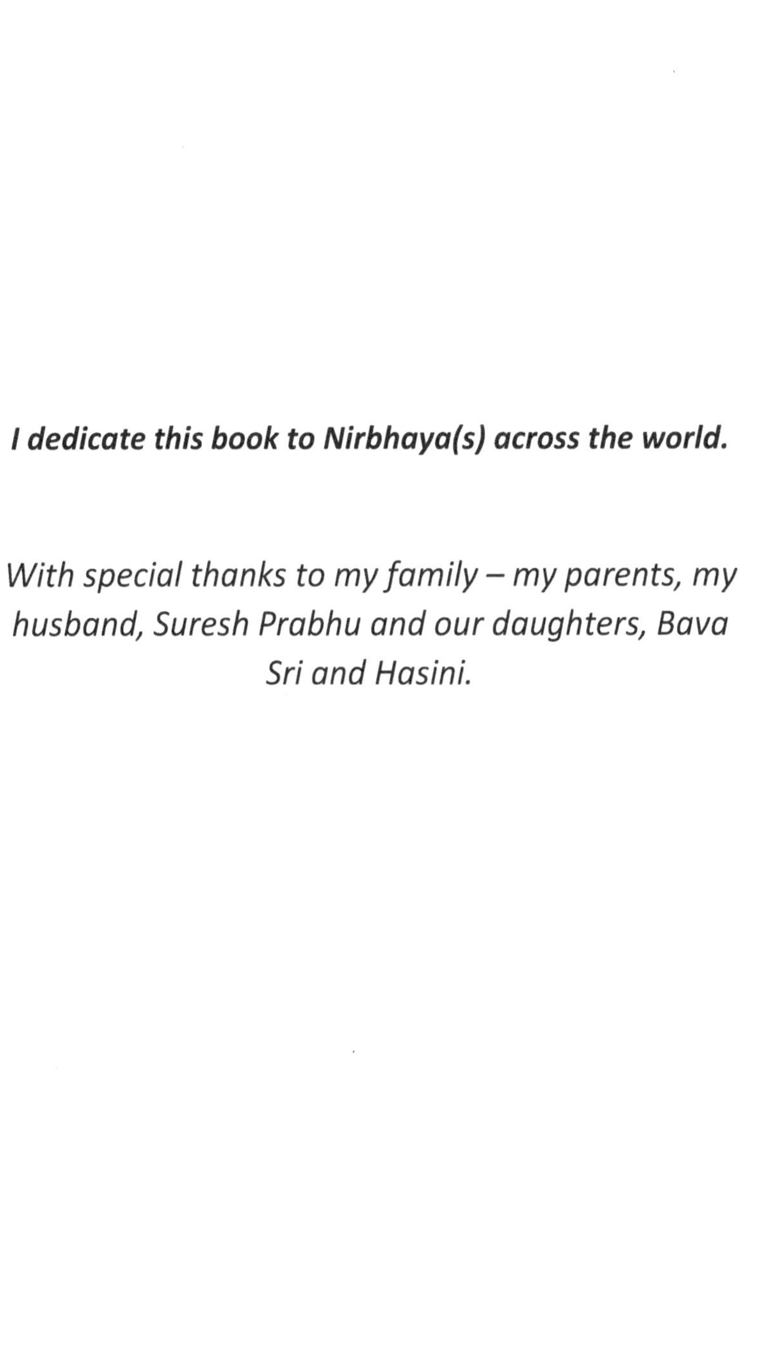

I dedicate this book to Nirbhaya(s) across the world.

With special thanks to my family – my parents, my husband, Suresh Prabhu and our daughters, Bava Sri and Hasini.

ABOUT THE AUTHOR

Ramya Ramalinga Moorthy is an IT entrepreneur with almost two decades of experience. She has worked with various leading MNCs. She is an Engineering graduate with Master's in Software Systems from BITS Pilani.

She is the author of Amazon Best Seller, *A Journey in search of* ~~SUCCESS~~ *Happiness* published in 2019.

She is the Founder and CEO of EliteSouls Consulting Services – a software testing firm that provides Quality Assurance, Performance Engineering and Cyber Security services. She is an aspiring writer and a motivational speaker. She enjoys learning and experimentation. She is passionate about inspiring others to live their BEST lives.

She is a proud mother of two adorable daughters and currently lives in Bengaluru, India.

Revenue from this book sale will be used by Ulaipal Uyarthuvom Charitable Service Trust towards educational and medical support for the needy.

Connect with Author:

Mail: ramya.happyjourney@gmail.com

YouTube Channel: Happy Journey - Lets Live Life

https://www.youtube.com/channel/UCXrDfkXUUksS9tiu8zlySIw/

Facebook Group: Inspirational Thoughts, Stories, and Experiences

https://www.facebook.com/groups/208784406925189/

ACKNOWLEDGEMENTS

I would like to express my gratitude to all those who reviewed and commented on the early versions of this manuscript to bring it to a better shape especially Krishna Raghav A C, Muthulakshmi S, Nivetha S, Raghuraman P, Thilagavathi R, Vasanthakumar P R, Vasuki R and Vijay Karthik N. This book would not be a possibility without their comments and critics.

My heart-felt thanks to editor, Kumari Smriti for her diligent evaluation. My special thanks to the entire publishing team. I am grateful to various women leaders who inspired me in my life, which triggered me to author this book. Thanks to all the online portals which helped me in my study about biographies of game-changer personalities and colour psychology.

I am highly grateful to my parents for imparting the importance of Navaratri celebration from my childhood days. The days that I have spent at the Durga temple every year during Navaratri since young age encouraged me to correlate the nine qualities required for modern women with the nine avatars. The actual temple mentioned in this book is the legendary Kondathu Kaliamman Temple located at Pariyur, near Gobichettipalayam in Tamil Nadu, India.

I am deeply thankful to my friends who supported and energized me as always. Last but not the least, my husband and kids, who willingly accommodated slash in my quality time with them to transform this dream book into a reality.

Ramya R. Moorthy

PREFACE

The 9 colours of Vibrant Women is an inspirational sequel of the book, *A Journey in Search of ~~Success~~ Happiness,* and it urges everyone to be strong and passionate to live a meaningful and extra-ordinary life. A teenage girl, Anila suffers depression after losing her school friend, in a sexual assault crime. Anila's loving mother, Shivani, tries to console her by detailing the key traits required for modern women - inspired by the 'Navaratri' celebration in their home town. Shivani educates her daughter to incubate nine different personality traits, by correlating each with the nine avatars of goddess Durga. These key traits emphasised for the well-being of women are presented by associating them with nine colours.

Shivani explains the need for SITUATIONAL SELF-LEADERSHIP to nurture our inner-self, that ensures our choice of trait be situation driven. Anila is finally convinced that the ability to choose and exhibit the right combination of traits in specific situations can help us face challenging situations in life. Inspired by her mother's analogy of nine avatars and colour references, what does Anila do as a tribute to her friend at the end? What was the impact of Shivani's discussions? That is for the readers to explore.

The book provides an agnostic message around the need for special personality traits in millennial women. With real-life examples of five exceptional women for each of nine colours, the book details forty-five inspirational stories of game-changers, to portray how a woman can lead a fulfilling life by pursuing their passion.

Though our Indian epics and literature portray women as the most respected individuals and our ancestors named rivers, nation, Gods, so forth by using feminine names, the present real life situation isn't very comforting. Not only our sophisticated lifestyle seems to have an upward trend, but the crimes against women, particularly sexual harassment of women and children, also seem to be on a rapid rise. This has brought shame to India despite our stupendous technological innovations and research outcomes.

As in case of any other social problem, addressing the issue at the root level is the best way to tackle it. The author feels that moral education (including public awareness and effective parenting) and severe punishment are the two key areas that need improvement to reduce sexual violence crimes against women. This book is an attempt to supplement the educational aids, by detailing different traits required for every woman to tackle the challenges in their life.

This book would serve as an inspirational aid for personal growth – to face life with courage and live up to our dreams to lead our BEST life by realizing our passion and potential.

Who should read?
Women, adults, teenagers and anyone who would like to understand the importance of women power and get inspired from Indian women game-changers. And for anyone who wants to have a fresh perspective into what being a woman could mean.

How to read?
The book contains various quotations, anecdotes and real-life stories of women personalities across various domains (deliberately excluded politics) to emphasize the traits described by the author. While reading about the nine traits, highlight the key sentences and read them several times till the desire to inculcate the trait within you is absolute. When you complete a chapter, come up with an action plan – baby steps to improve the qualities within yourself. This will help you become the most aspired form of YOURSELF.

Let's Appreciate the Power of Women!!

TABLE OF CONTENTS

About the Author - - - - - - - - - - - i

Acknowledgements - - - - - - - - - - - iii

Preface - - - - - - - - - - - iv

Chapter 1: Expect the Unexpected - - - - - - - - - - - 3

Chapter 2: Enthusiasm, Socialism and Success - - - - - - - - - - - 13

Chapter 3: Simplicity, Calmness and Inner-Peace - - - - - - - - - - - 23

Chapter 4: Passion, Strength and Courage - - - - - - - - - - - 34

Chapter 5: Responsible, Reliable and Honest - - - - - - - - - - - 45

Chapter 6: Warmth, Happiness and Optimism - - - - - - - - - - - 56

Chapter 7: Growth, Health and Harmony - - - - - - - - - - - 67

Chapter 8: Authority, Maturity and Neutrality - - - - - - - - - - - 80

Chapter 9: Care, Compassion and Hope - - - - - - - - - - - 92

Chapter 10: Creative, Grandeur and Wisdom - - - - - - - - - - - 104

Chapter 11: Situational Self-Leadership - - - - - - - - - - - 115

Chapter 12: The Advent of Justice - - - - - - - - - - - 126

Women Personalities Index - - - - - - - - - - - 138

Appendices - - - - - - - - - - - 141

Chapter 1

Expect the Unexpected

" You've got to expect things are going to go wrong. And we always need to prepare ourselves for handling the unexpected."

\- Neil Armstrong

I was heart-broken and hopeless. I was cursing the society for being irresponsible. I never thought our neighbourhood was so cruel and unsafe. I questioned myself a thousand times, how could this happen? Everyone around me seemed bewildered. I was starving for positive news, as my hearing aid was tired of receiving sobbing sounds. Everyone around me had a thousand unanswered questions running through their mind.

I was standing twenty feet from the ICU. I couldn't control my emotions. I remembered my mom's words, 'Everything happens for a reason', but I couldn't convince myself about that. I didn't have energy left to cry loudly, anymore.

Doctors weren't confident about the possibility to save Nirbhaya as her intestine was badly damaged and she had lost a lot of blood. I was shattered and had no tears left. It had been almost three days waiting outside the ICU without food or sleep. Every heart beat tried to assure me by saying, "No, this is someone else, not my dear school friend, Nirbhaya."

I wasn't this devastated, even when I found that I had become permanently deaf, when I was twelve. My accidental deafness was nothing compared to what had happened to Nirbhaya.

At the sound of Nirbhaya's mother calling for me, my heart beat shot up. Nirbhaya was looking for me. Words can't explain my state when I walked in to see Nirbhaya. As my tears fell on her hands, she slowly opened her eyes, with great difficulty. Her facial expression and tears spoke a thousand words about what had happened to her inside the bus though she couldn't utter a syllable. My heart was torn into pieces looking at her condition. I kissed her palm, that had bite marks, and said, "Don't worry dear, everything will be alright soon."

When I opened my eyes, I saw my mom sitting next to me. I looked around and realized I was in our hometown, in Tamil Nadu, and two days had already passed. My mom hugged me and narrated what had happened. She had brought me home after I fainted inside the ICU. As per doctor's advice, I was given sleeping dose along with intravenous saline drip. I was recommended complete bed rest for a few days.

For the next couple of days, I kept pestering my mother with hundreds of questions. Not sure whether she purposely avoided my queries or simply didn't have an answer - she often requested me to remain calm. She kept sharing some of the safety measures to be followed while going out, but hardly anything seemed to filter through my ears.

She conveyed this more than twenty times – *Always expect the unexpected and be prepared to handle the UNEXPECTED with courage. Learn to be proactive and vigilant always.*

She said in sad voice, "The crimes against women are rising. The entire society has to be blamed for such incidents. To an extent, everyone became selfish and busy in their lives so much, so that compassion towards others took a backseat. Government cannot arrange bodyguards for everyone. Society needs to take equal responsibility and object, if someone misbehaves with someone at a public place. The problem stems not just from those men committing these crimes, the blame lies with everyone who allows such incidents to happen. We all became busy in our rat race to gain materialistic wealth, not bothered about what is happening around us. For many of us, the extent of our service to society is limited to sharing awareness messages in WhatsApp group or on other social media platforms.

Despite the rise of sexual crimes against women, the social status of Indian women has exponentially improved in this era. Women have carved their name in every profession that were once deemed as male dominant. You need to look at them as role-models to fulfil your life purpose. The contemporary situation about women's safety will be soon sorted out."

But still I couldn't believe the gang rape and brutal torture undergone by Nirbhaya by the team of monsters inside a moving bus. I couldn't accept the fact that, according to the National Crime Records Bureau, every 15 minutes, a child is sexually abused in India.

To expect the unexpected shows a thoroughly modern intellect.
- Oscar Wilde

As my third semester holidays were going on, it wasn't a big challenge for mom to plan this short vacation to our home town. But I knew it would definitely be tough for my dad and my brother Ajay, to manage without my mom's support. Living in Bengaluru, the Silicon Valley of India, we were all used to the self-absorbed city lifestyle. May be that's why, I have a great love for our home town, a beautiful village with rich lush green farms surrounded by mountains all around. This is my mother's birth place. The village has many famous movie shooting spots. Ajay and I love to roam around our farm in a two-wheeler and visiting our relatives in nearby villages. Indeed, it's a great place filled with rich people. I mean people with a big heart not in terms of materialistic wealth.

The next morning, I woke up at 7 a.m. by the chirping sounds of birds. When I stepped out of my room, I was surprised to see the festive mood at home. I looked around for mom to know what special day it was. I called my grandmother but she was in a hurry to clean the pooja room. She asked me to take bath quickly and help her with decorations. She wanted me to help her arrange the clay idols in the wooden stand (Golu[1]) and make flower garlands. I heard from her that mom was in the backyard, plucking flowers for pooja. My grandfather, who was reading newspaper murmured, "Today is the first day of Navaratri[2]. Go and take bath quickly, and then we will have breakfast together."

I knew Navaratri is one of the popular traditional celebrations in my home town. Without wasting more time, I went back to my room to get ready. I decided to divert my mind from my musings and spend time with my grandparents that day, to have a peace of mind. Though my grandparents strictly follow traditional beliefs and customs, they always believe in gender equality.

During our breakfast, I asked, "Grandpa, did ancient Indian women enjoy social rights?"

"As per our history, Indian women's social status has seen many ups and downs. With many forces working against and for her, her destiny has seen wide variations since ancient times.

---

[1] Golu refers to the festive display of clay dolls and figurines in South India during the autumn festive season, particularly during Navaratri (Dussehra / Dasara). These displays are typically thematic.

[2] Navaratri is a Hindu festival that spans nine nights (ten days) and is celebrated every year in the autumn. It is a celebration of victory of good over evil though it has different rituals followed in various parts of India.

During the Rig Vedic period (1500 B.C to 500 B.C), women enjoyed equal status with men. This was the era when feminine forms of Hindu Goddesses were believed to be born. This was the golden period for women. Girls and boys were equally educated. The Vedas state that an educated girl should be married to an equally educated man. Many educated women became poets, teachers and philosophers. In that society, women took active part in agriculture, in manufacturing bows and arrows, and, in weaving cloth, among others; hence enjoying economic independence.

Then, came the age of Dharma Sastras (2nd century B.C), which created a lot of setbacks in women's status. Seclusion of women was introduced and the freedom enjoyed by women earlier was gradually taken away from her. Women's position in family and in society became low. Women were treated as child-bearing machine and child marriages were encouraged.

Then, the Buddhist age (3rd century B.C to 6th century A.D) wiped away the discrimination and exploitation of women. This period came as a boon to women and created a series of positive changes in their lives. Women education was encouraged and child marriages were considered as an offence. But Buddhist age failed to achieve gender equality in everyone's mind.

After the decline of Buddhism (3rd century A.D to 12th century A.D), during the pre-medieval period, the situation turned worse again. During Medieval period (12th century A.D to 16th century A.D), the caste system became more rigid. In general, post Buddhist period, confusion prevailed and women's status deteriorated drastically. Social movement of Indian women was restricted and women were always portrayed as dependent on their husbands. Women were illtreated and considered socially inactive. Women were denied all intellectual and spiritual development. Women became economically dependent on men and they accepted they were inferior to men. Many social evils like female infanticide, sati, purdah system were developed during this time. Polygamy contributed further to this downward turn and there was no limit set to the number of wives for a man. And also dowry system became popular.

Later, during the British rule (1757 to 1947), many Indian reformers joined hands and worked hard relentlessly to destroy some of the evil practices against women. This led to betterment of women. As Mahatma Gandhiji himself was victim of child marriage, he very well knew the immorality of such a custom, and hence urged to boycott child marriage. After India's independence, women's social status started improving slowly. Indira Gandhi served as Prime Minister of India for fifteen years.

Feminist activism gained momentum in late 1970s and it led to several improvements in women's economic and social status. With the formation of several women-oriented non-profit organizations, there was significant advancement made in women's rights. This led to social improvements, although restricted to urban areas. Each day, we see more women coming forward and making history across all professions. However, when it comes to women safety, the situation has only deteriorated in the last few decades.

The Government of India declared 2001 as the *'Year of Women's Empowerment'*. But according to a poll conducted by the Thomson Reuters Foundation in 2001, India was the "fourth most dangerous country" in the world for women. Still rural Indian women are undergoing several challenges to lead their life. They are starving for supporting platform to bring them out of the social malpractices. I am scared that the situation doesn't go down further and hope things will improve," said grandpa.

After breakfast, I started helping my grandmother in decorations. My grandmother is a simple women and a very good story-teller, even better than my mother. She liked my creative idea to make beautiful four feet long garlands. My grandmother usually makes

4 or 5 beautiful garlands, to decorate the goddess' statue at our nearby Durga temple, on all nine days of Navaratri. It is a ritual followed from mom's childhood days. After we finished making garlands, we cleaned and arranged the Golu as per the theme recommended by my grandmother.

As I enjoy hearing stories from grandma, I purposely asked her, "Grandma, what is special about Navaratri?"

"How come you forgot our Navaratri celebration?" questioned my grandmother. I simply smiled at her, insisting to know more, to pull her into the story-telling mode.

She began, "Hinduism is more than a religion. It is a culture, a way of life. India is the land of powerful women. Indian epics and literature have evidences that woman power destroyed kingdoms. No one can forget the legendary Tamil women, Kannagi, who bravely protested against the Pandyan king for the injustice done to her husband at the king's court. She cursed the king and their capital city, Madurai, to be burnt. She is still worshipped as a goddess in some regions of India and Sri Lanka.

Veda Vyasa's Mahabharata is a story about the fall of Kauravas as they humiliated queen Draupathi. Valmiki's Ramayana is a story about destroying king Ravana who abducted king Rama's wife, Sita.

Navaratri means 'nine nights'. It is a festival spread over nine nights. This celebration signifies the 'WOMEN POWER'. Our ancestors always had a great faith in goddess Durga, the mother of all beings that exist in this world. Each night of Navratri is dedicated to different avatar of goddess Durga. Devotees celebrate supreme feminine energy and worship her wholeheartedly to get her blessings during these nine nights.

Durga is a Sanskrit word meaning 'inaccessible fortress'. She is considered as the guardian who takes us through difficulties and who is beyond defeat. Each avatar of Durga is special and portrays different qualities of goddess Durga. Worshiping her on these nine nights, we will get her blessings to live a blissful life.

Navaratri signifies the victory of goddess Durga over Mahishasura, the buffalo demon. Mahishasura got a boon of being indestructible and started misusing his power. As he harassed others, goddess Durga fought against him and defeated the demon in the war that took place for nine days. She killed him to bring back world peace. To represent this, the tenth day is celebrated as Vijayadashami to worship the weapons and celebrate the success.

As Navaratri is a celebration of victory of good over evil, we spend these nine nights worshipping goddess Durga for our well-being. As the evening dawns, we visit temples and neighbours' home to enjoy singing devotional melodies. We exchange gifts and homemade foods."

I could sense grandma's faith and respect towards goddess Durga in her voice.

In the noon, I asked mom, "Do you believe in the Navaratri story shared by grandma?"

"Listen Anila, there is nothing wrong in our ancestor's beliefs and rituals. You need to understand the fact that there is a vital message hidden inside every ritual reinforced by our ancestors. But in order to keep it simple and easy to understand, sometimes the real meaning is either hidden or some elaborate tale is spun to strictly instil the practice. So, you need to interpret the real meaning behind this ritual.

Different forms of the supreme feminine energy are celebrated to remind every woman what they are actually capable of. Every woman should get inspired from the nine avatars of goddess Durga to face life situations audaciously.

Remember, Navaratri is our national festival, celebrated across many states in India for various reasons, and thus through different rituals. Celebration of Navaratri or Dussehra, as it is called in some parts of our country, has two major anecdotes around it. Firstly, to celebrate Lord Rama's victory over the Lankan king Ravana, who kidnapped his wife, Sita. Secondly, goddess Durga killed Mahishasura, a demon. Both the reasons reflect the war that happened during these nine days and their VICTORY is celebrated as the victory of good over evil.

I don't look at Navaratri as a religious festival of Hindus. Rather, I consider it a ritual to be practiced by everyone in the world. These ten days are the best days to cleanse oneself and improve our personality as a human being.

I prefer to interpret the Navaratri celebration this way - As night usually helps us to take good rest, we wake up every morning feeling refreshed. Similarly, these nine nights of Navaratri are the best time for deep rest to clear up our mind, spend time for self and revitalize ourselves. These nine nights are our best chance for deep relaxation, prayers, meditation, fasting, etc to feel refreshed. In spiritual term, this is the time to unite us with nature, the Universe, and feel our SOUL. Let's discuss more at bed time tonight.

As you have completed 18 years, this is the best time for you to learn some of the key traits required for a modern vibrant woman. I want you to realize the real message behind Navaratri. There is something to learn from each avatar of Durga which is very important for every woman to lead a blissful life. I would like to share with you my interpretation, of how I look at Navaratri."

My mom wound up quickly as she wanted me to take a short nap. I slept thinking about the two different point of views, that of my grandmother and mother.

Expect the unexpected, believe in the unbelievable, and achieve the unachievable.
- Anonymous

In the evening, I dressed in traditional attire. We all had good time singing hymns and worshipping alongside our relatives and neighbours. After finishing the evening pooja at our home, my grandparents and I started heading to the nearby Durga temple in our car. Though it is just a 15 minutes' drive from our home, my grandfather never allows me to drive his car due to safety reasons. My mom stayed at home as we expected some of our relatives and neighbours might visit our home until late night. As soon as the car started, my grandma recited me the speciality of that day.

Chapter 2

Enthusiasm, Socialism and Success

" Mere colour, unspoiled by meaning, and unallied with definite form, can speak to the soul in a thousand different ways."

- *Oscar Wilde*

" **T**he first day of Navaratri is considered to be very auspicious. This night is dedicated to Shailaputri, the first avatar of goddess Durga. Being born to the king of mountains, Himavan, she is also known as Parvati and Hemavati. She is the absolute form of Mother Nature. In her previous birth, she was Sati, the daughter of the great king, Daksha. Sati disobeys her father and marries Lord Shiva. Daksha considers this a personal insult, and to show them down does not invite them for a grand yagna that he organizes. But Sati attends the ceremony ignoring her husband's advice, for the love of her father. After arriving at her maternal home, she feels uninvited and when Daksha insults her husband in front of all the esteemed guests, she blames herself. As she couldn't abide the insult, she burns herself in the holy fire of the yagna. Hence, in the other birth, she is born as Hemavati and marries Shiva. The goddess is depicted having a crescent moon on her forehead, carries a trident and a lotus in her hands while sitting on a bull. She gives fervour and victory to devotees who worship her. As she symbolizes earthly existence and success, today's pooja will begin with a ritual that symbolizes women power," said grandma.

We reached the temple. I was awestruck with the beautiful floral decoration on goddess Durga statue. I could sense the pride in my grandmother's face as her flower garland highlighted the decoration making it perfect. I met a few of our relatives and old friends and had good time listening to devotional songs.

We returned home at around 8 p.m. I went to my room after having delicious dinner, served with love and laughter. I saw a small gift on the bed with a handwritten note, "Do you have ORANGE colour traits? It's time to explore within you. Act now." I quickly opened the gift. It was a beautiful orange colour crystal which had the inscription - ***"Enthusiasm, Socialism and Success"***.

I then realized the reason, why mom gifted me the orange colour attire that evening. While I was still exploring the crystal, admiring it at different angles, mom entered the room. I asked her, "Mom, is there any relation between these words and this orange crystal?"

"Yes Anila. You guessed right. ORANGE is the colour of SUCCESS. This orange crystal represents the traits like enthusiasm, courage, socialism, positive attitude, and confidence to lead a successful life. The orange colour traits are very important for a woman to stand out in the crowd and lead an enthusiastic and successful life.

Success is walking from failure to failure with
no loss of enthusiasm.
*- **Winston Churchill***

Generally, these women are highly enthusiastic, agile, friendly, aspirational, adventurous and independent in nature. This colour is full of positive energy and represents qualities like warmth, inspiration, and determination to succeed. Pursuing your choice without getting biased by others' opinion and being successful in whatever you are passionate about is important for your well-being.

Deepa Malik is a proud Indian athlete who proved that her disability was not a show-stopper in achieving her life ambition. She was born in Sonipat, Haryana. Being an army officer's daughter and wife, she never let her spinal tumour to end her active life. The 3 surgeries and almost 200 stitches helped her get rid of the tumour but paralysed the lower part of her body. Nevertheless paralyses could not take away her courage to bag many awards in the sports arena. She has won more than 55 national and 20 International medals across various sports like javelin throw, discus throw, and shot put.

She operated her catering business for 7 years, to manage her family needs and to take care of her two daughters. When Deepa's husband was fighting at Kargil War as a army officer, she was fighting with her tumour at home. The family won both the wars. She had a turning point in her life at the age of 36 when she decided to pursue a career in sports. In an interview, Deepa said that when she was struggling to manage her family, her father's words, *"It's always better to light a lamp than to curse the dark. You become the change you want to see like Mahatma Gandhiji..."* influenced her to realize the bigger purpose in her life.

She is the first Indian woman to win a medal in Paralympics in the women's shotput F53 event at the 2016 Summer Paralympics at the age of 45. She is also a motorcycle racer. Government of India has honoured her with the prestigious Rajiv Gandhi Khel Ratna award, Arjuna award and Padma Shri.

Not everyone can muster such ZEAL to break barriers through their hard work, determination, strength and will power. She is the best example of an enthusiastic and successful woman in Indian history.

In India, often women give up their passion and career aspirations after marriage or after having children. And in some cases, even if a woman is interested to pursue her desire despite managing her personal commitments, not every family renders whole-hearted support to her. She is either called irresponsible working mother, unfit for family life or a woman who runs behind money.

But beyond all these restrictions, there are a few courageous women who live their lives to satisfy themselves ignoring others' certification. They understand that it doesn't matter to be in everyone's good books. They keep their motivational level and morale high to pursue their dream even after having children. For such women, definitely every day will be unique and messy with unforeseen challenges. But their ENTHUSIASM and SOCIALIZING SKILLS would help them overcome sensitive challenges both at workplace and at home. They believe in planning and working hard instead of 'good luck'. Definitely, it is not a cake-walk, but only those brave vibrant women, who managed their struggles with positive attitude and determination, became successful in life.

Pranjal Patil, born in Jalgaon in Maharashtra, lost her vision completely when she was six years old. Though she became completely vision impaired, her blindness never stopped her from becoming India's first visually-challenged woman IAS officer and obtain a PhD in International Relations.

Her interest in civil services helped her clear Union Public Service Commission (UPSC) exam with All India Rank (AIR) 773. She was allotted a job in Indian Railway Accounts Service (IRAS) but later the offer was revoked due to her vision impairment. This rejection made her stronger and motivated her to reappear for the exam the following year and achieve AIR 124.

While preparing for the UPSC exam, she used a screen reading software with Braille display. Also, Pranjal had to find a suitable writer who could match with her dictation speed. But these hurdles couldn't hamper her enthusiasm to ACHIEVE her goal.

Immediately after her training, she took charge as Assistant Collector of the Ernakulam district in Kerala. She became Sub-Collector of Thiruvananthapuram, Kerala in 2019. She says, *"Success doesn't give inspiration; the struggles behind the success gives the inspiration."*

---

*To be successful, the first thing to do is to fall
in love with your work.*
- Sister Mary Lauretta

Irrespective of their gender, children who grow up in tough financial situation, their struggles INSPIRE them to accomplish big things. Particularly girls brought up in such family environment are aware that *'Success is a continuous journey and not a specific destination'*. They continue to think big and move forward enthusiastically stomping on their failures as stepping stones to lead their SUCCESSFUL life.

Dr. Bani Yadhav, the fastest Indian women rally driver, was born in Lucknow and grew up in Gurgaon. She is the first Indian woman to be awarded with an International Doctorate in Motorsports.

Though Bani identified her passion towards racing at the age of 13, but after marriage, she had to sacrifice her interests to manage her family's financial situation. Only after raising her children and becoming financially secure, she started her racing career again in 2013. She had a major spine injury and underwent 2 back surgeries. But her winning attitude made her to recover and brought her back to the track within 6 months.

In an interview, she said, *"If you really want to empower yourself, believe in yourself. Live your dreams and don't let anyone define your worth."*

She has won prestigious titles like first woman to receive Asia Cup – IRC rally Championship and first woman to receive FMSCI – Outstanding Woman in Motorsports Award for rallying for the year 2016. She was a forty-five year old mother of two, yet the first Indian woman to drive a Formula 4 car at the Yas Marina Track in Abu Dhabi in 2016. She was awarded with the Best Sportsperson Award 2017 by Haryana State Government.

There are no secrets to success. It is the result of preparation, hard work, and learning from failure.
- Colin Powel

In India, except in urban areas, not many families bring up their girl child by emphasizing on the need for them to have a successful career. Unfortunately, career is always considered optional for them. Most girls don't get a chance to casually socialize with their neighbours or relatives, so they develop inferiority complex from their childhood days.

EDUCATION is the important missing attribute in most of such cases. Until this situation changes, the crimes due to women's ignorance would continue. At least in cities, children grow up in the environment with gender equality, imparting the need for being successful in a career of their choice. This has led to equal respect for both sexes. Every parent should take immense care to seed this strong message from their childhood days. This will create successful women leaders.

Indra Nooyi is the former CEO of PepsiCo, consistently ranked among *The world's 100 most powerful women* in Forbes magazine. She currently serves on the board of Amazon and International Cricket Council. Born in Chennai, Tamil Nadu, Nooyi completed her graduation in Madras Christian College and Indian Institute of Management in Calcutta. She then got her master's degree in Public and Private Management from Yale University in USA.

During the initial period, though she received financial aid from Yale, she had to work as overnight receptionist to manage her financial needs. She couldn't afford to buy a formal suit to attend interview at business-consulting firms. But she had a clear vision and enthusiasm to achieve it.

Known for her high energy and hard working attitude, Indra had held various positions at Johnson & Johnson, Boston Consulting Group, Motorola and ABB before joining PepsiCo in 1994. She led and restructured PepsiCo's global strategy. She also took the lead in the acquisition of Tropicana, Quaker Oats and others, which raised the net annual profit of the company from $2.7 billion to $6.5 billion. She became the CEO of PepsiCo in the year 2006 and served for 12 years. In her 24 years of service at PepsiCo, she introduced more healthy products to the company's food and drink portfolio. During her tenure, the company's sales grew 80%.

She was honoured with Padma Bhushan by president of India. She was ranked the 2nd most powerful woman on the Forbes list of *The 19 Most Powerful Women in Business.* She holds honorary doctorate degree from various universities.

In a magazine interview, she said, *"I wake up in the middle of the night and write different versions of PepsiCo strategies on a sheet of paper."* Indubitably, she is one of the best CEO and role-model for many entrepreneurs.

Your positive action combined with positive thinking results in success.
— Shiv Khera

How many times, have you wondered looking at a woman in her 40s and 50s and wondered how young and energetic she looks? The secret of their physique and energy level is actually their POSITIVE THOUGHTS. They are the women who love to SOCIALIZE with others and easily bring big positive change in their life and in the environment around them. They knew how to keep themselves away from toxic people, who would bring down their positive vibrations. They were careful about choosing right environment and friends to spend their quality time.

Arunima Sinha is a mountain climber and sportswoman, born in Ambedkar Nagar in Uttar Pradesh. In 2011, she was mercilessly thrown out from a running train as she resisted against the robbers from snatching her gold chain. She fell on the parallel train track where another train crushed her left leg below the knee. She raised funds through various sources to get an artificial leg. She is indeed a brave hearted woman who became unimaginably stronger and courageous after this incident, and chased her dream nevertheless.

She took 18 months mountaineering course and climbed Mount Everest with her prosthetic leg. She became the first female amputee in the world to reach the summit of Mount Everest in May 2013. She never believed in destiny, rather believed in herself.

In 2014, her book, *Born again on the mountain – A story of losing everything and finding it back* was launched by Prime Minister of India. This book is about her unforgettable story of hope, courage and resilience.

She had also scaled Mount Elbrus in Europe, Mount Aconcagua in Argentina, Mount Kosciuszko in Australia, Mount Kilimanjaro in Africa and Carstensz Pyramid in Indonesia. In 2019, after climbing the Mount Vinson in Antarctica, she accomplished her goal to hoist the national flag of India on the highest peaks of all seven continents.

She was honoured with Padma Shri and Tenzing Norgay Highest Mountaineering Award to name a few. She was conferred with the honorary doctorate by the University of Strathclyde, UK. She is an inspiration to amputees around the world. Her fortitude and enthusiasm awarded her the real success that she deserves.

Nothing great was ever achieved without enthusiasm.
- Ralph Waldo Emerson

On this first night of Navaratri, I want you to think about these qualities of a vibrant woman. Even if you don't see a path, own a winner's attitude to CREATE a new path to pursue your passion. Surround yourself with like-minded people and socialize with them. This will help you push yourself, even if you lose faith at times due to failures. I want you to incubate ORANGE colour qualities within yourself. Be enthusiastic, social and successful to lead your best life," concluded my mom.

Socializing is more positive than being alone, that's why meetings are so popular.
- Mihaly Csikszentmihalyi

It was a highly inspiring discussion with my mom about orange colour traits. I requested my mom to return to Bengaluru as I knew it would be difficult for my dad and Ajay to manage without her physical presence. And also as Ajay was in twelfth grade, considering his studies, I couldn't afford to be selfish and make mom stay with me at our home town. Though they were all absolutely fine with the current situation, I wasn't comfortable with this decision.

With great difficulty, I managed to convince my mom to return, after I told her that I was feeling guilty and couldn't have peace of mind due to this plan. My mother promised me to send me a gift for the next eight days and agreed to speak to me every night at 9 p.m.

The next morning, I woke up early to help my grandma in preparations for pooja. I helped my mother pack her trolley. She returned Bengaluru in the noon.

After finishing the evening pooja at home, grandma and I visited a few of our neighbours' houses. Then, along with my grandfather, we quickly got into the car to visit the temple. We were in a hurry as we were running late for the aarti[3]. My grandmother never misses the 7 p.m. aarti at the temple during these nine Navaratri days. We headed to the Durga temple.

------

[3] Aarti is a Hindu religious ritual of worship, a part of pooja, in which light (usually from a flame) is offered to one or more deities. Aarti also refers to the songs sung in praise of the deity, when the light is being offered.

Chapter 3

Simplicity, Calmness and Inner-Peace

" The soul becomes dyed with the colour of its thoughts."

- Marcus Aurelius

" **T**he second day of Navaratri is dedicated to goddess Brahmacharini, an avatar of Durga. She is the meditative form of goddess Durga and portrays - leading a simple and conscious life. She ignores every discouragement and faces all the struggles to pursue her desire. She does Tapasya for several thousand years to convince Lord Shiva to marry her. After seeing her determination and extreme penance, Lord Shiva accepts her. Goddess Brahmacharini is considered as the mother of austerity. She acts as the storehouse of knowledge. She is worshiped to develop mastery over the mind, body and soul. The goddess is depicted as bare footed, holding a rosary in right hand and water utensil in left, which symbolizes bliss. She enlightens us with knowledge, love, inner-peace and divine grace," said grandma.

We had a great time in the temple. I returned home with great curiosity about the gift. As I was gifted with beautiful white attire, I guessed I would have discussion with my mother, on white colour that night. I quickly finished dinner and went to my room. On my bed, I saw a small gift along with a handwritten note, "Do you have WHITE colour traits? It's time to explore within you. Act now." I opened the gift and it was a beautiful transparent white crystal which had the inscription - ***"Simplicity, Calmness and Inner-Peace"***.

Before I could even type a 'thank you' note to mom, I received an audio message from her at 9 p.m. sharp. I quickly tapped on the message to open it.

WHITE is the colour of SIMPLICTIY and PERFECTION. This transparent white crystal represents attributes like being simple, calm, humble, self-contented and having inner-peace to lead a meaningful life. As you know, white has equal balance of all colours. Understand that life is also full of various kinds of situations. You need to learn to accept the reality and stay positive in all circumstances in life. It is very important to be simple and humble whatever you achieve in life.

---

*Kindness is the language which the deaf can hear
and blind can see.*
– Mark Twain

Generally, these women are very simple, and carry down-to-earth humbleness and great human values. They work as per their heart desires rather than what their brain says. The white is a colour known for innocence, purity, calmness and cleanliness.

Sudha Murthy, a social worker, author and philanthropist was born in Shiggaon in Karnataka. She was the only female among 599 students in her engineering college. She is a gold medallist in her master's degree in Computer Science at Indian Institute of Science, Bengaluru. She was the first female engineer hired by TELCO (Tata Motors).

The advice received from J.R.D. Tata changed Sudha's perception towards life – *"If you make lots of money you must give it back to society as you have received so much love from it."*

She is the wife of Narayana Murthy, the founder of Infosys Limited. In 1996, she cofounded Infosys Foundation, a non-profit organization that provides support for rural development, and education and healthcare for the under privileged section of the society. Through her foundation, she spreads the awareness for rural education, public hygiene and poverty alleviation. The foundation has built more than 10,000 toilets in rural Bengaluru and funded 70,000 libraries for Indian schools.

She took a pledge at Kashi temple to give up shopping and buy only essential items. According to her, this gave her a sense of freedom and helped her listen to her conscience. She always dresses in simple cotton sarees, never gives importance for her physical look and known for her simplicity.

She is one of the renowned authors of India. Her passion towards charitable activities made her write stories on general lives expressing her views on charity. She has written several books in English and Kannada which are based on her real-life experiences. She has received many prestigious awards like Rajyotsava award, Raja-Laxmi Award, Lifetime Achievement award and Padma Shri for her social works.

In one of the interview, she said, *"I believe women are more courageous than men. Women should know their potential and harvest it for their betterment..."*

There are two ways to be rich : one is by acquiring
much and the other is by desiring little.
— Jackie French Koller

I want you to believe that beauty of a woman lies in her heart - in her THOUGHTS. Unfortunately, in this decade, there is an exponential increase in a harmful trend - women have started giving much importance to physical look and costumes. Despite the fact that increased usage of cosmetics have led to many new skin diseases, many get addicted trying 'to look beautiful'. There is nothing wrong in the intention to look elegant. But sometimes, it is unnecessary. For example, during our Indian marriages we notice a majority of women would get dressed up, sometimes even more than a bride, which I feel unnecessary. By taking wrong inspiration from movies, they end up dressing boorishly. Unfortunately, they end up becoming a trend setter inspiring others to blindly follow their way to maintain their social status.

You need to clearly understand the real sense of beauty. Be SIMPLE. Luxury lifestyle doesn't mean that you need to spend lavishly to enhance your physical appearance. These might give momentary pleasure but cannot get you a everlasting happiness. Instead, be HUMANE by contributing to charitable organizations. This act will make you more beautiful. Let such acts prove you are leading an affluent lifestyle not your attire or makeup.

We can't forget **Mother Terasa**, a Roman Catholic nun who dedicated her life to serve the poor. She lost her father when she was eight-years-old and her mother raised her with deep interest and passion towards charity. When she turned eighteen, she decided to become a nun and serve the poor. On her arrival to India, she began to work as a teacher and later became the principal at an educational institute in Kolkata. During that time, she had a calling that transformed her life. She wanted to start a home to help the poor people in the city.

She founded 'Missionaries of Charity' which is a Roman Catholic religious institute to care for the hungry, sick and homeless people who felt unwanted and unloved, and were abandoned by the society. She lived her life by her words, *"Not all of us can do great things. But we can do small things with great love"* - inspiring several million people around the world. She expanded her work to several other countries. She received numerous recognitions including, Bharat Ratna, the highest Indian civilian award. She was honoured with the Nobel Peace Prize and became a symbol of charitable, selfless work. In 2016, Mother Teresa was canonised by the Roman Catholic Church as Saint Teresa.

Peace is the only battle worth waging.
– Albert Camus

In the name of westernization, never tend to dress up in a way that makes only you comfortable. Your dress should also make others around you comfortable. I am not saying to dress-up only in traditional wears but at the same time remember there is a thin line between being modern versus being vulgar. Wrong inspirations drawn from movies and television shows are invariably giving rise to this trend which ultimately leads to people using it as a reason to tarnish the image of women and in some extreme cases commit social crimes against women. You need to remember the importance of our traditional values. Your dress should never affect your VALUES.

Lata Mangeshkar is one of the best known Indian playback singer, and music director, who has sung more than 50,000 songs in 36 Indian and foreign languages. She was born in Indore city in Madhya Pradesh and was interested in music since young age. She started acting in her father's musical plays at the age of five and learned music from her father. She did not receive a formal education as she did not attend school.

She started her journey of being a professional singer at the age of 13. She has sung songs in different genres for several music directors. Though, she faced many rejections initially, later her voice gained popularity in film industry. Lata sang a patriotic song, about Indo-China war on Jan 27 1963, that brought tears to the then Prime Minister of India, Jawaharlal Nehru. She has been the sweet voice behind many actresses for four generations but she hates doing makeup. Known for her simplicity and humbleness, she always keeps herself away from fashion.

She has received numerous awards and honours. She has received three highest civilian awards - Padma Bhushan, Padma Vibhushan and Bharat Ratna. On her 90th birthday, she was honoured with the title, '*Daughter of the Nation*' by the Prime Minister.

Simplicity reveals the pure beauty of life.
– Debasish Mridha

There are many women who have left their high paying jobs in the interest to serve the society. For them working for a social cause gives them bigger satisfaction than gathering materialistic wealth. They aren't bothered by giving up worldly pleasures; instead they fight for the welfare of the SOCIETY. They ignore their physical appearance, rather work hard selflessly for social welfare. They get immense sense of SATISFACTION and INNER-PEACE in their social activities. For them wealth or fame isn't more important than their personal satisfaction.

Shaheen Mistri is a social entrepreneur who was born in Mumbai but grew up in different countries as she moved with her father who was a banker with a multi-national bank. She holds Masters in Education from the University of Manchester.

When she returned to Mumbai as a young college student, she walked into Mumbai slums and expressed her deep desire to teach the under privileged children. Her interest in the education of economically backward children urged her to become the founder of Akanksha Foundation at the age of twenty. This non-profit organization works on a mission to impact the lives of low-income communities by providing education to their children.

She is the CEO of Teach For India (TFI) since 2008, a non-profit organization that addresses the issue of educational inequity. The organization encourages college graduates and young professionals to spend time in teaching in low-income schools. TFI currently operates in Mumbai, Pune, Chennai, Bengaluru, Delhi and Hyderabad. It has expanded from serving 15 children in a centre to more than 4,500 children in 50 centres and 15 schools in Mumbai and Pune during the last twenty years.

She says, *"Our children showed me that hope is the colour of transformation in the face of great difficulty."* She has authored a book, *Redrawing India: The Teach for India Story*, which portrays the power of personal reflection of the work by Teach for India fellows and staff. She has received the title of *Global Leader for Tomorrow* at the World Economic Forum.

As a woman of noble thoughts, Shaheen inspires others to follow her work, *"It shapes you and gives you more than you could possibly imagine."*

Inner-peace begins the moment you choose not to allow another person or event to control your emotions.
*— **Pema Chodron***

The secret for inner-peace is to ensure all the negative thoughts are replaced by positive ones. These women valued the inner-peace more than the billions they could earn in their life. They learnt and practiced how to develop inner-peace amidst the life storms. SELF-EXPLORATION helped them to identify their life purpose. The clarity in their vision gave them determination to achieve their goals. They learnt that getting freedom from worldly pleasures and selfish desires alone can get them peace of mind.

Indu Jain, the eighty four years old entrepreneur, an educationalist and a philanthropist is the chairperson of Bennett Coleman & Company Ltd (BCCL) that owns The Times Group, one of the largest media house in India.

She was born in Najibabad, Uttar Pradesh. In 1838, BCCL was founded and established in Mumbai by Ram Krishna Dalmia; later on managed by his son-in-law Sahu Shanti Prasad. As a member of Sahu jain family, Indu inherited their legacy business. Their media house publishes renowned newspapers and magazines including The Times of India, The Economic Times, Femina and Filmfare. It also manages various TV and radio channels. The Times group publications are currently run by Indu's sons.

Her dedication and hard work has made the Times Group as one of the largest media industries. Known for her simplicity, Indu created the Times Foundation to bring a positive difference in the society, for which she has received many national and International awards. The foundation focuses on various community services and research. Their Times relief fund provides financial support towards disaster relief efforts on cyclones, earth-quakes, epidemics, etc.

She is a humanist and spreads the message of inner-peace through various conferences. She is a spiritualist and has addressed the United Nations in the Millennium World Peace Summit 2000 – a gathering of religious and spiritual leaders. She is very active in women empowerment activities.

She serves as a chairperson of the Bharatiya Jnanpith Trust, a literary and research foundation that presents India's highest literary awards. According to her, 'being happy' and 'identifying the life purpose' are not two different things.

She was conferred with the Padma Bhushan in 2016. She has been awarded with the prestigious Lifetime Achievement Award 2019 by the Institute of Company Secretaries of India (ICSI) for Translating Excellence in Corporate Governance into reality.

Your calm mind is the ultimate weapon against your challenges.
— Bryant McGill

These women never gave importance to their physical appearance rather they worked hard for a social cause which made them special and beautiful. They remind me of Swami Vivekananda's response to an American who asked him, "Can't you wear proper clothes to look like a gentleman?" Vivekananda smiled and politely replied, "In your culture, a tailor makes a gentleman; but, in our culture, CHARACTER makes gentleman."

On this second night of Navaratri, I want you to think about these qualities to become a vibrant woman. You should experience inner-peace and your inner thoughts are more important in life than your physical appearance or materialistic wealth that you create. Always be humble and strive hard to beautify your thoughts not your external appearance. I want you to incubate WHITE colour qualities within yourself. Be simple, calm and content with what you have been blessed with to lead a blissful life.

*The smallest act of kindness is worth more than
the greatest intention.*
– Kahlil Gibran

The audio stopped.

This message from my mom made me to realize the real meaning of beauty and the importance of being modest. I winded up my day with thoughts about the beautiful women who worked for social cause and upliftment of the society.

The next morning, I woke up early and continued the routine activities - helping grandma in cleaning the pooja room and arranging the clay idols as per third day's theme.

That noon, my old friend, Vanitha came home along with her father, Captain Dharmaraj. Dharmaraj uncle is an ex-army man who actively took part in the Kargil War. He is a good friend of my grandfather. Vani was brought up by her grandparents as her mother passed away in an accident, when she was 10 years. I took Vanitha to my room and we started talking about our childhood experiences.

And then we started talking about our current lives. I knew she had started a new job in Bihar. But when I enquired about it, I found out that she quit her industrial job within 6 months of joining and returned home. I was shocked to hear that her decision to resign was due to sexual harassment and threats made by her supervisor.

She said, "Only those in my team who agreed to all his requirements were allowed to continue on the job." Unfortunately, Vanitha didn't share this issue with her father thinking it might tarnish their family status. I requested her to share this with her father, so that the culprit could be punished for his bad behaviour. But, Vanitha wasn't convinced. She said she wasn't emotionally strong to tackle the issue now, but promised me that she would share this with her father once she is ready. They left after a few hours.

I still couldn't comprehend why women shy away from sharing the truth to punish the culprits. I was lost in thoughts as I realized sexual violence against women has become an epidemic that requires immediate solution.

After finishing the evening pooja at our home, we got into the car and headed to the Durga temple.

Chapter 4

Passion, Strength and Courage

" The greatest masterpieces were once only pigments on a palette."

-   Henry S. Hoskins

" The third manifestation of goddess Durga is Chandraghanta. She carries a crescent moon on her forehead. After Lord Shiva agrees to marry goddess Parvati, on their wedding day, Shiva reaches king Himavan's palace in a terrorizing form with the marriage procession of gods, mortals, ghosts, ghouls and sages. As her mother and other relatives faint in terror, to avoid further embarrassment to her family, Parvati transforms herself into a terrorizing form – Chandraghanta. She is portrayed having golden complexion with three eyes and ten hands, each holding a weapon, and sitting on a lion. With her third eye always open, she gives an ever fighting posture to destroy demons. She then persuades Shiva to transform into a pleasing form. Shiva accedes and reappears as a prince to marry her. She shows passion, vigilance and readiness to battle evil from all directions. Devotees worship her to be blessed with strength and audacity," said grandma.

That day, I did meditation in the temple for an hour along with my grandmother and returned home feeling re-energized. As I was gifted with red attire that day, I was prepared to learn the qualities of red colour from my mother. While having dinner I noticed a small gift parcel on the dining table. I quickly grabbed it and rushed to my room to open the gift. I saw a handwritten note on my bed, "Do you have RED colour traits? It's time to explore within you. Act now." I opened the gift and it was an attractive red crystal which had the inscription - ***"Passion, Strength and Courage"***.

I couldn't take my eyes off the beautiful crystal and at sharp 9 p.m., I heard a beep from my mobile. It was an audio message from mom. I tapped on the message.

RED is the colour of PASSION and BRAVERY. The red crystal conveys valour, heroism and vigour to fight against the hurdles in order to pursue your passion. There will be tough situations in your life but you need to be resilient and brave to face all the struggles with perseverance and win the game of life. Red traits will give you the necessary power to face challenges with heroism.

Strength does not come from physical capacity.
It comes from an indomitable will.
– Mahatma Gandhi

Generally, these women are passionate, fearless, mentally strong and resilient, and possess high energy level. Red is a dominant colour, with longest wavelength, as it is at the end of visible spectrum of light. As red is the colour of blood, historically it has been associated with danger, though in modern world, red reflects passion, fortune and love.

By design, every woman has a great mental STRENGTH. Scientific research has indicated that women can handle stress and tough situations better than men. Unfortunately, not every woman realizes her inner strength. Women should be aware of their inner power during challenging times to fight and succeed in a battle.

Being successful doesn't necessarily mean defeating the opponent, it also refers to RISING UP after a failure and supporting others to overcome similar situation in their lives.

Sometimes when you're in a dark place you think you've been buried, but you've actually been planted.
— Christine Caine

Laxmi Agarwal is the acid attack survivor who said, *"I had nothing to feel ashamed of. I decided not to feel sorry for myself, instead survive and lift my life myself to tell my story so that no one else faces a similar situation."*

The acid attack incident took place in Delhi market, in 2005, when Laxmi was fifteen years old. It disfigured her face and other body parts. This attack was a revenge for her refusal to marry her friend's brother. Laxmi was mentally broken and she had to undergo seven surgeries in a span of seven years. She stayed under a blanket for months as she wasn't even able to wear any clothes.

But she developed courage to emerge from darkness. She took her case to court and after 4 years, the attackers were sentenced to imprisonment. She filed a Public Interest Litigation (PIL) in the Supreme Court for the total ban of acid; and in 2013, court imposed restrictions in the sale of acid. Laxmi also became a key campaigner for Stop Acid Attacks.

She instituted Chhanv foundation, in 2014, to help the survivors of acid attacks. Through her foundation, she counsels the patients about the right procedures to follow in case of an attack and assists in rehabilitation and legal aid. She was honoured by Michelle Obama with the International Women of Courage Award, in 2014.

She has received International Women Empowerment Award 2019, for her Stop Sale Acid campaign.

In an interview, she said, *"My attacker thought he would leave me trapped in my house."* She became one of the best examples for mental strength and courage to tackle challenging situations.

Strength does not come from winning. Your struggles develop your strengths. When you go through hardships and decide not to surrender, that is strength.
– Arnold Schwarzenegger

Women should always be ready to face life struggles BOLDLY. Sometimes, tough situations might drive you to unknown and unexplored horizon. During such times, every woman should realize the hidden power inside them to BRAVELY face the roller-coaster ride of life. Believe you are born to bring a big change in this world and become a role model for handling misfortunes. This thought will help you push yourself to get onto the positive track.

Avani Chaturvedi is the first female fighter pilot of Indian Air Force (IAF) to fly a solo fighter jet. She hails from Rewa district, Madhya Pradesh. Her family's army background helped her to follow her passion. At the age of twenty-four, she completed her training at Hyderabad Air Force Academy and completed her solo flight in a MiG-21 Bison fighter aircraft.

Earlier, she had flown solo in aircrafts like the Pilatus PC-7 turboprops, Kiran and Hawk jet trainers. She, along with Mohana Singh and Bhawana Kanth, were the three women officers to be inducted into the Indian Air Force fighter squadron in 2016. She was honoured with a doctorate degree from Banasthali Vidyapeeth.

In 2018, she was promoted to Flight Lieutenant. Her passion and courage has helped her etch her name in history, in this male-dominated profession. Avani became a great inspiration to many young women, when she flew the super-sonic fighter aircraft, known to have the highest take-off and landing speeds.

Avani broke the stereotype, 'Combat, by nature, is a male occupation' and said in an interview, *"The best part of being a pilot is that you are flying an aircraft—it is a machine. The aircraft does not know who is sitting behind it, so the machine will behave in the same way it would behave with a male pilot."*

Passion is energy. Feel the power that comes from focussing on what excites you.
— Oprah Winfrey

Explore your life purpose and be PASSIONATE to bring your dreams into reality. Always remember, only 10 percent of your life is not in your control, the remaining 90 percent is all about how you REACT to the life situations. Be courageous to face the challenges and become a game changer in life. Being brave doesn't mean you need to take a sword or knife to stop the crimes happening around you. You need to voice out the problems and bring it to the public forums to take legal actions.

Sometimes, all you need is to be PROACTIVE and avoid unnecessary challenging situations. Sometimes, be smart by ignoring your unworthy rivals - they might not deserve your attention. And sometimes, during worst case life-threatening tough situations, do not hesitate to take a sword to safe-guard your life and to serve justice.

Nusrat Khan Pahade a survivor of sexual harassment during her childhood, a mother and social activist started the Cactus

Foundation to raise awareness and fight against child sexual abuse. As she herself had undergone such terrible incident, she bravely came forward, determined to voice against child sexual abuse.

She travels around schools to teach children the difference between 'good' and 'bad' touch for safe childhood. Nusrat believes that when it comes to making kids understand about sex and sexuality, most parents just want to brush it under the carpet.

Through her organization, for the last 16 years, volunteers who are mostly homemakers are working hard to create awareness around the issues faced by children. They educate children on different acts of sexual abuse and create awareness about the *Protection of Children from Sexual Offences Act*. This has helped children voice their concerns about such issues with parents or teachers, instead of keeping quiet or feeling shy to share it.

By working with parents, teachers and children, Cactus foundation creates opportunities to create a better ecosystem for children to understand the importance of such issues that are otherwise avoided. Their emphasis on "break the silence" urges children and adults to speak up about such crimes.

Follow your heart, listen to your inner voice,
stop caring about what others think.
– Roy T. Bennett

Women undergo lot of sensitive challenges be at workplace or at home throughout their life. Some of the challenges cannot be solved but they need to sail through them with courage and a positive attitude. Fortunately, these struggles give women an exponential strength and make them fault-tolerant. As a modern women need to play different roles, both at home and workplace, they need to adapt to the ever changing environment. At the same time, they need to be straight forward to openly share their thoughts and point of view. Unless, you be COURAGEOUS and come forward to speak about your problem with your parents or friends without carpeting it, you will not be able to lead a peaceful life.

Kriti Bharti is a social activist, rehabilitation psychologist and child marriage warrior of India. She herself comes from a troubled childhood, but she had the courage to rise up and earn a doctorate in psychology from a University in Jodhpur. She had taken an oath to dedicate her life to save young children. According to UNICEF, India leads in the number of child marriages in the world, with about 40% girls are married before the age of 18. And the state of Rajasthan tops on this issue.

In 2011, Kriti established the Saarthi Trust, a non-profit organization in Rajasthan to prevent child marriage by educating girls about their rights, and protecting the victims. According to her, *"child marriage is a 'dark room' where children cannot see into the future"*. Through her organization, she educates girls to create awareness and to know about their rights. Saarthi Trust has annulled more than 30 child marriages and prevented over 900 child marriages.

After realizing the fact that just annulling a child marriage does not end the problem, she has setup a rehabilitation programme, by helping these girls with their basic needs, including education. This creates opportunities for the former child brides, and prepares them to face the society and to lead a successful life. She delivers training in many schools, colleges, police academies and administration offices in Rajasthan. In spite of facing criticism and death threats, she continues to save girls to brighten their life. She is indeed a great inspiration for women to follow their dreams with courage.

Kriti's first annulment of a child marriage in India was recorded in the World and National Record books. Her courage, determination and contribution to abolish child marriage and rehabilitate girls has inspired many young women in India.

You cannot swim for new horizons until you have courage to lose sight of the shore.
– William Faulkner

When situation demands, don't think twice to break the rules and FOLLOW your heart. Never lose YOURSELF in the interest of satisfying others' interest. These women never bothered about society's credit rather followed their heart and worked for themselves. If you follow this, success will be yours. These women knew that they were SOLELY responsible for bringing their dreams into reality. So, they never gave up that opportunity to others or tough situations to win over them.

Remember, YOU are born to WIN. You are born only after a big biological win inside your mother's womb. And more importantly realize that even if you fail, the real winner is the one who has the courage to rise up and continue the game of life with additional vigour. These women live as per Swami Vivekananda's inspiring slogan, *"Arise, Awake, and stop not until the goal is reached."*

Rani Rampal, the captain of Indian Women's Hockey team was born in Kurukshetra, Haryana. Her father was a cart-puller. Despite hailing from a poor family background, her determination to follow her passion helped her. She became the youngest player, at the age of fifteen, to represent India in Women's World Cup. From a very young age, Rani aspired to uplift her family situation. She identified her interest at the age of 6 and became the International hockey player at the age of 14.

She met Baldev Singh, a Dronacharya award-winner coach at Shahabad Hockey Academy who supported her to transform her dreams into reality. Rani is the only Indian player to be named as the Best Young Player of the Tournament in women's World Cup 2010. In the same year, during Commonwealth Games, she was nominated for FIH's Young Women Player of the Year. Her strategies made India win a bronze medal in the Hockey Junior World Cup in 2013. In 2018 Asian Games, she led her team to win a silver medal for India. She was honoured with Arjuna award.

In 2007, Rani suffered from a major back injury that left her bedridden. As she became very weak, doctors and trainers told her that's the end of her career. But she refused to give up and recovered from it. Certainly, it's her PASSION that helped her overcome all hurdles in life. In 2009, she played in the Champion's Challenge Tournament held in Russia and was declared, *The Top Goal Scorer* and The *Young Player of the Tournament.*

She is the best example to realize the fact that POVERTY gives an exceptional strength and courage to face difficult times and ignites a fire to achieve big success in life.

To succeed, you have to believe in something
with such a passion that it becomes a reality.
– Anita Roddick

Strive hard and never hesitate to travel an extra mile to pursue your PASSION. Doing the work that you are passionate about would give you the driving power to travel an additional distance in every task. FOCUS on your goals and be determined to meet your targets no matter how tough the situation turns out to be.

On this third night of Navaratri, I want you to think about these qualities to become a vibrant woman. Be brave to face the failures and don't be afraid to break the rules whenever required. It's okay not being in everyone's good books but don't compromise on your dreams. This will help you to lead your fearless life. Pursue your passion. I want you to incubate RED colour qualities within yourself. Be passionate, have mental strength and live life with courage.

Success is not final, Failure is not fatal; It is the courage to continue that counts.
– Winston Churchill

The audio stopped.

I could sense a huge positive energy course through me after hearing the audio message from my mom. The discussion helped me to assess whether I have explored myself thoroughly to identify my life purpose. I took a oath that I will never step back until I achieve my vision. I couldn't sleep for next couple of hours as my thoughts wandered around those women who courageously fought to bring their dreams into reality.

The next morning, I woke up early and supported my grandma in making the garlands. As our maid aunty and I started arranging the clay idols as per third day's theme, we casually started talking about our past celebrations and family members. I was distraught to know that her husband got paralysed from waist down a few years back. In order to reduce her family's financial needs and manage the crises, she made her daughter quit her studies in ninth grade to support her father at home. Whereas, her son continued his studies in a private school.

I understood from her that when they approached for help, my grandmother has asked them to move to our outhouse and made her daughter to continue her school despite the break. Also, my grandmother has warned and stopped her daughter's marriage arrangements.

I wasn't clear why she made her daughter to stop her studies. Instead she could have made both her children to study in a government school instead of spending for her son's education at private school. She didn't had a convincing answer when I questioned her why there is a partiality shown towards boy child.

I was concerned why a girl child's education is considered optional and why there is a gender inequality even within a family. I felt this could be the reason why boys don't develop mutual respect towards girls from their young age. My grandmother shared me some of the myths prevalent about girl child education at their village and insisted the need for nation-wide awareness for not only mandating girl child education but also parental education to treat their children with gender-equality.

After finishing the evening pooja at our home, three of us headed to the Durga temple.

Chapter 5

Responsible, Reliable and Honest

" **T**he fourth day of Navaratri is dedicated to goddess Kushmanda, an avatar of Durga. This form is the happiest manifestation of the goddess. The word 'Kushmanda' refers to 'creator of little cosmic egg'. The glow and radiance from her body is luminous as that of sun and she is believed to have created the Universe. With her smile, she brought light to the dark cosmos. She is the source of all energy and resides inside the sun. She is believed to provide direction to Sun God. Like other forms of Durga, she is depicted with eight hands holding lotus, rosary, jar of honey and blood, sword, bow, arrow, chakra and mace. She rides on a tiger symbolizing elegance and strength. She is the creator of three supreme goddesses – Mahakali, Mahalakshmi and Saraswati. She provides great qualities to mankind. She blesses her devotees with well-being, values, wealth and power to fulfil their responsibilities," said grandma.

We had a pleasant time at the temple. After we returned home from the temple, I sensed a great feeling of satisfaction and faith in myself. As I was gifted with blue attire that day, I was prepared to hear from my mother about blue colour attributes. After dinner, I entered my room and noticed a small gift parcel along with a handwritten note, "Do you have BLUE colour traits? It's time to explore within you. Act now." I opened the gift and it was a magnificent blue crystal which had the inscription - *"Responsible, Reliable and Honest"*.

I quickly grabbed my mobile and tapped on the audio message received from mom.

BLUE is the colour of RELIABILITY and HONESTY. The blue crystal represents traits like being trustworthy, honest, loyal and intelligent. It insists to live by these core human values. Blue signifies tranquillity yet strong and powerful energy. Living a life by following a great value system is important to lead a purposeful life.

*Integrity is the most valuable and respected
quality of leadership. Always keep your word.*
– Brian Tracy

Generally, these women are trustworthy, elegant, highly responsible, intelligent, honest and reliable. They are known for their INTEGRITY - even during challenging situations, they never compromise on these key values. They are magnanimous and are known for their wisdom, authenticity and elegance.

Indu Malhotra is the first female lawyer appointed as Supreme Court judge in 2018, after working as Senior Advocate for thirty five years. She made history as the first women to be elevated to this role directly from the Bar Council of India rather than being promoted from a High Court.

She was born in Bengaluru and followed her father's footsteps to get into law. She completed her master's in Political Science and worked as a Political Science lecturer for a while. Later she pursued Bachelor of Law and joined the legal profession in 1983. She secured first rank and became qualified as an Advocate-on-Record in Supreme Court - a feat for which she received Mukesh Goswami Memorial Prize. She became the Senior Counsel at the Supreme Court in 2007.

She is an expert in arbitration, and has appeared in various domestic and international commercial arbitrations. She is a member of the Vishakha Committee on Sexual Harassment of Women at the Workplace. She has been conferred with various honours for her work. She became the second woman to be designated as Senior Advocate by the Supreme Court in 2007.

Since its inception in 1950, till date, a total of 229 people have been appointed as judges in the Supreme Court of India, but only 6 of them are women. In 1989, Justice Fathima Beevi became India's first female Supreme Court judge. Today, the court has three women judges, Indu Malhotra, Indira Banerjee, and R. Banumathi among its 34 judges. It is a big accomplishment for every Indian woman to feel proud of, as it is a traditionally male dominant field.

Honesty is the first chapter in the book of wisdom.
— Thomas Jefferson

These women never believed that they were not capable or eligible to choose any profession. They just required a supportive environment to bring their dreams into reality. Only a fraction of women who get support from family or who face tough challenges early in life take charge of their life to make history. But majority of the women decide to forego their aspirations to live for others.

They are the ones who need to realize their POTENTIAL thereby their life purpose to FULFIL their destiny. They should stop living in their comfort zone to fulfil their responsibilities and to achieve their vision.

Tessy Thomas, the 'Missile Woman of India' is the first woman scientist to head a missile project in India. She is known as Agni Putri (one born of fire) for her exceptional work as the leader of missile project. She joined Defence Research and Development Organisation (DRDO) in 1988 and was appointed to work on the Agni missile programme by Dr. APJ. Abdul Kalam. She gradually became the Project Director of long range nuclear missiles, Agni-IV and Agni-V. In 2018, she became the Director-General, Aeronautical Systems of DRDO.

Born in Alappuzha, Kerala, she grew up near Thumba Rocket Launching Station. The rocket station fascinated her and created in her the interest towards space research. She lost her father at a young age, and had to take educational loan to do her Engineering. She secured a scholarship that helped her cover the tuition fees. Her family situation didn't stop her from pursuing master's and PhD in Guidance Missile.

In 2006, a missile failed and her team had to face a lot of criticism. But Tessy, tenaciously took it as a challenge and within ten months, the faults were corrected and she turned the failure into another success.

She is the recipient of Lal Bahadur Shastri National award for her contributions and excellence in the field. She has received several awards for her work including DRDO Scientist of the year and Outstanding Woman Achiever Award, to name a few.

If you realize your responsibility, you will realize your destiny.
– Tasneem Hameed

A woman's biggest responsibility is not just to get married and take care of her family. Personally, having a family is very important, but she can lead a happy life only if she can BALANCE her career aspirations and personal life. Unfortunately, due to social folklores, many women think they cannot take care of their family if they pursue their passion. This has led to increase in graduate mothers quitting their job after having children. It's high time that these women realize the fact that those women game changers who made history also had a happy family. They just learned to be smart to maintain work-life balance.

We all have the same 24 hours in a day, but they learnt to PRIORITISE their tasks which made them to fulfil their responsibilities. Effective time management skills helped these women to excel in their personal life and career. For many successful women, core values like TRUSTWORTHINESS and HONESTY become their success secret.

Dr. Kamala Selvaraj is a pioneer in infertility treatment. She is an obstetrician and gynaecologist from Tamil Nadu who commissioned the first test tube baby of south India in 1990. She did her PhD in Reproductive Physiology and was awarded the distinction of First Research Scholar in Reproductive Physiology in Tamil Nadu. She was awarded doctorate for her thesis on *Premature Ovarian Failure and its management.*

Thirty years ago, childless women were illtreated and considered unlucky, by their family members and society. That was the time, Kamala helped many women by providing them with alternate child birth solutions. She brought happiness in many women's lives. More than 800 babies were delivered as a result of assisted reproduction therapy conducted by her hospital. She provided free treatment to those mothers who lost their children in the 2004 Indian Ocean tsunami.

She has published several research papers and books. She has received many awards including Rajiv Gandhi Memorial National Integration Award, Jeevan Bharathi Award, and Lifetime Achievement Award to name a few.

Reliability is the hallmark of a dignified personality.
– Rajendra Muthye

Most successful women identify their life purpose very early in their lives. They face challenges but their attitude towards obstacles helps them manage tough times and excel in their career. The clarity in their thoughts amplifies their VISION to achieve their goals amidst the struggles. They were always reliable and took complete ACCOUNTABILITY of their job.

Everyone has challenges in life, but those who turn them into OPPORTUNITIES - win, and those who gave up to their hurdles - fail. All of us face both happy and sad times in our life. But during tough times, compromising on a few things based on our priorities, but not losing our peace of mind can help us achieve our dreams.

These women worked hard to maintain a winning positive attitude to live their best life. They remind me of Dr. APJ Abdul Kalam's words, *"All birds find shelter during a rain. But Eagle avoids rain by flying above the clouds. Problems are common, but attitude makes the difference!"*

Kiran Bedi, a retired IPS officer and social activist, is the first women IPS officer of India. She is currently serving as the Lieutenant Governor of Puducherry. She served India for 35 years and took voluntary retirement after serving the post of Director General of the Bureau of Police Research and Development.

She was born in Amritsar, Punjab. She obtained her PhD in Social Sciences from IIT Delhi for her research on 'Drug Abuse and Domestic Violence.' From a young age, she had great interest in social upliftment.

She completed her training and got her first posting as IPS officer in the year 1975. That year, in the Republic Day Parade, she became the first woman to lead an all-male contingent. While in charge as Traffic Commissioner of New Delhi, she brought in spot fine rules and clamped down errant motorists and towed improperly parked vehicles using cranes. She didn't spare even the car of former Prime Minister, Indira Gandhi. This earned her a nickname as 'Crane Bedi.'

Kiran's seven year old daughter who suffered with Nephritis was sick and required to undergo continuous treatment. Despite her daughter's health condition, she had to shift to Goa, and thereafter other locations, due to the transferable nature of her job. Her family had to stay in Amritsar, so she managed travelling between these places to fulfil both her role – as a mother and a police officer.

She held several key positions in her tenure. As an Inspector General of Prisons, she introduced a number of reforms in the management of Tihar Jail. She was awarded with an honorary degree, Doctor of Law in acknowledgment of her *"humanitarian approach to prison reforms and policing."* She has been one of the active members of Anna Hazare's anti-corruption movement.

She was awarded with a UN medal for her outstanding work with them. She has received many awards including Pride of India Award, Mother Teresa Award and Lifetime Achievement Award to name a few.

Leadership is about vision and responsibility, not power.
— Seth Berkley

These women, with their HARD WORK and DETERMINATION, made our nation proud of them. If you get into each of their personal lives, you'll see that they had to overcome many tough challenges and make many compromises but they were all dedicated to their career. They were highly RESPONSIBLE to meet their job expectations. Only their passion and positive thinking, in spite of personal life challenges, helped them live a meaningful life as per their dreams. A few women even lost their lives bravely while working on their passionate career - they lived with great DEDICATION to pursue their passion and died with a great satisfaction and hence made history.

Kalpana Chawla, the first Indian-American women to go to space was born in Karnal, Haryana. She was interested in aeroplanes even as a child. She completed Aeronautical Engineering from Punjab Engineering College, India and pursued her master's and PhD in USA.

She began her work at NASA's Ames Research Centre on computational fluid dynamics research. In 1991, she became naturalized American citizen and joined NASA Astronaut Corps. For her first space mission in 1996, she along with six crew members flew Space Shuttle Columbia. She was the primary robotic arm operator and deployed a satellite that studied the outer layer of the sun.

In 2001, she was selected for her second flight and returned to space through Space Shuttle Columbia. She along with her crew performed about 80 experiments studying earth and space science. Unfortunately while returning to earth, Chawla and six other astronauts died due to spacecraft crash. She died at an early age of 42.

She has logged 30 days in space over the course of her two missions. After her death, she was honoured with the Congressional Space Medal of Honour, NASA Space Flight Medal and NASA Distinguished Service Medal. In 2004, *The Kalpana Chawla Award* was instituted by the Government of Karnataka to recognise young women scientists.

Kalpana is indeed a great example for every woman to realize the hidden power inside them. She is an inspiration to THINK BIG and achieve big. Mother India is proud of such a brave woman. Like her, every woman is highly powerful by design but they just need to realize it and act upon it.

The price of greatness is responsibility.
– Winston Churchill

As per Swami Vivekananda's perspective, while developing values for oneself, one should first focus on those qualities that make us a strong person and then start adding qualities that will make sure we will do good acts. Most of the game-changer personalities who lived their best life had followed core values like honesty, compassion, generosity, responsibility, passion, social service, etc. It's these VALUES that actually helped them to successfully achieve their vision; not materialistic wealth.

On this fourth night of Navaratri, I want you to think about these qualities to become a vibrant woman. You need to identify, and practice great values and live as per your core VALUE SYSTEM. Keep up your words and do what you have promised. Take complete accountability for all the consequences of your actions without blaming others. Consistently work with determination carrying a winner's attitude to cross a hurdle. The rest will be taken care of by the Universe. Learn to be tenacious and resilient to meet your life's purpose. I want you to incubate BLUE colour qualities within yourself. Be responsible, reliable and honest to lead a PERFECT life.

Integrity is doing the right thing, even when no one is watching.
– C.S. Lewis

The audio stopped.

I was awestruck after hearing about the passionate women and their achievements. I wanted to salute these brave women who contributed to the society disregarding their personal pleasures. They had a fire in them which made them work for the community instead of focussing only on their family.

The next morning, I woke up with ambitious thoughts, as it had been great experience learning about women game changers who didn't stop with looking after their family, but also worked for uplifting the society.

It was a usual day of garland making and setting up pooja room. At noon, my aunt, who is a renowned doctor at the government hospital in our village, came home. Mrs. Anupama, my mother's school friend is a highly passionate woman. She completed her post-graduation in medicine with distinction. I have a great respect for her.

But when she started talking about women's current status in India, her words disconcerted me. She said, "Most of the sexual violence crimes against women are caused due to their dressing style, behaviour, carelessness... That is the root cause of this problem."

Before I could interrupt her, my grandmother quickly stopped her and said, "No, Anupama. I disagree with your point of view. It may be so in a few cases. I agree the crimes do sometimes happen due to bad inferences made from few women's behaviour and their irresponsible dressing style. But it is not acceptable to give such a generalized statement against women based on exceptional cases.

We cannot blindly point at a woman's behaviour or attire as the excuse for such crimes. Think about how many sexual violence cases against toddlers have been reported in recent years, where the innocent kids were brutally raped and murdered.

A percentage of women, unfortunately from educated sector, they tend to misuse their freedom. Sadly, these women wrongly take inspirations from movies and other entertainment channels and dig their own grave. These women require moral education to understand the real meaning of women empowerment and freedom.

Unknowingly they contribute to life-threatening situations towards other women in the society. If these women can be educated through parental support, definitely the situation will improve. Basically they need to understand the need to carry forward our Indian women's cultural values to next generations. If they are made aware of this responsibility and the moral values carried by our ancestors, this issue could be addressed."

After a long discussion, my aunt finally aligned herself with my grandmother's thoughts. Though my grandmother isn't educated, that day I realized that the value system she carries has helped her raise her children successfully.

We finished the evening pooja at our home a bit early and headed to the Durga temple.

Chapter 6

Warmth, Happiness and Optimism

" Clouds come floating into my life, no longer to carry rain or usher storm, but to add colour to my sunset sky."

- Rabindranath Tagore

" The fifth manifestation of Durga is goddess Skandamata. She is depicted as a mother holding the infant Lord Karthikeya on her lap and with four hands, holding lotus and bell in her arms, riding a ferocious lion. She is referred to as 'Goddess of fire.' The demon, Tarakasura gets a boon from Lord Brahma that only Lord Shiva's offspring could kill him. Tarakasura assumed Shiva, who practiced austerity, would never marry anyone. Soon he started misusing his powers and troubled all the gods. Later, Shiva and Parvati marry and produce a powerful seed, which is grown at Saravana Lake, nurtured by six mothers. Even as a child, Karthikeya showed exceptional valour and warfare skills, leading him to be chosen by gods as the commander in chief for the war against evil forces, and he finally kills Tarakasura. Goddess Skandamata is worshipped as the mother of supreme child. As a mother, she is kind and awards devotees with divine happiness, power, optimism, salvation and prosperity. Those who selflessly worship her will attain their ambitions and acquire treasures in life," said grandma.

We spent an hour in the temple and returned home. As I was in yellow attire that day, I knew that my mother would share about qualities of yellow colour. I quickly finished my dinner and went to my room. I sensed a cool breeze from the open windows. I noticed a small parcel near the window along with a handwritten note, "Do you have YELLOW colour traits? It's time to explore within you. Act now." I opened the gift and it was an appealing yellow colour crystal which had the inscription - ***"Warmth, Happiness and Optimism"***.

By the time, I grabbed my mobile and sent thank you note to my mom; I received the audio message from her as it was already 9 p.m.

I pulled a chair and sat near the window. There is a big banyan tree just outside my room, fresh air came in and nourished my body and soul. I felt lighter and relaxed. I tapped on the audio message.

YELLOW is the colour of OPTIMISM and HAPPINESS. Yellow is the colour of sunshine. The crystal conveys the need for cheerful thoughts and happiness within us. It is associated with positive energy, intellect, joy and incomparable optimism. It is one of the most powerful colours, easily visible and the first colour kids respond to. It is considered a warm colour that keeps us energetic and cheerful.

Happiness is not something readymade. It comes from your own actions.
— Dalai Lama

Generally, these women are known for their cheerful nature and optimistic thoughts. They are very positive, energetic, passionate and brave. They care for their personal well-being. Their strong belief in themselves gets them all that they aspire in life.

Bhakti Sharma is the first youngest Asian women swimmer to create a record in Open water swimming in Antarctic waters. She set a world record by swimming 1.4 miles in 41.1 minutes, at a temperature of 1 degree, breaking previous world record. She is only the third person in the world to swim in the Arctic Ocean, and recently become the youngest swimmer to conquer all five oceans of the world.

She started swimming at the young age of two and a half, coached by her mother, who was a national level swimmer herself. Bhakti was born in Mumbai and brought up in Udaipur. She participated in several state and national level championships. In 2003, when she was 14 years old, she did her first Open Water Sea swimming for 16 kilometres from Uran port to Gateway of India.

Bhakti along with her mother-cum-coach Leena Sharma and friend Priyanka Gehlot, formed a three member women's relay team, that holds the Asian record for their swim across the English Channel. Bhakti and her mother also share a world record of being the first mother-daughter duo to swim across the English Channel. She was awarded with the Tenzing Norgay National Adventure Award from the President of India.

The young swimmer's achievements weren't without struggles - her parents had to take loans, multiple times, to finance her travel expenses. In spite of swimming not being much acknowledged sport in the country and the financial struggles, she was able to give her best to bring her dream into reality. She dreams to win gold medal for India in 2021 Tokyo Olympics.

At the end of the day, personal satisfaction and happiness are important to live a FULFILLING life. Bhakti and her parents are a good example and inspiration for dreamers - *Dream gifts us a special power to turn it to a reality*. No doubt, Bhakti's mother is a pillar of strength and reason for her daughter's success. They serve as a good example to realize that happiness is our choice that comes by following our passion and not from the external world. Afterall, HAPPINESS is something to be realized internally in our hearts.

The pessimist sees difficulty in every opportunity. The optimist sees opportunity in every difficulty.
— Winston Churchill

P. T. Usha, a retired athlete was India's first woman to take part in the finals of an Olympic event. She is a well-known Indian women athlete.

She was born in Meladi, Kerala in a poor family. Despite the poverty and lack of nutritious food, she performed exceptionally in sports. Her talents were identified at a young age and she was trained by the coach O. M. Nambiar. She started her International career as a sprinter in the Moscow Olympics, 1980. Since then, she has won more than 100 national and International medals, and is referred to as *'The queen of Indian track and field'* and nicknamed 'Payyoli Express.'

Her poverty was never an excuse for her performance on the ground. She has won 13 gold medals in Asian Championships. In 1985, Usha was deemed as the best women athlete at the Jakarta Asian Meet where she was regarded as sprint queen as she won 5 gold medals and a bronze medal.

In 1983, she was honoured with Arjuna Award, and in 1985, she was conferred with the Padma Shri. She was named 'Sportsperson of the Century' by the Indian Olympic Association and awarded with Adidas Golden Shoe. Currently she runs an athletics school and coaches aspiring athletes to win medals for India. One of her trainee, Jisna Mathew, has won two Gold medals at Asian Junior Athletics Championship in 2016.

Usha's optimistic thoughts and enthusiasm to pursue her passion became her success secret. She realized AUTHENTIC HAPPINESS lies in doing her passionate work. After giving birth to her son, she returned back to the track with a gap of 4 years and won a silver medal at the Hiroshima Asiad. She is the best example to realize the fact - follow your passion to achieve highest level of happiness in life.

The key to being happy is knowing you have the power to choose what to accept and what to let go.
— Dodinsky

Those who learnt to COUNT THEIR BLESSINGS achieved big things in life. They always acknowledged that what was given to them and felt blessed, though they consistently tried to improve themselves. These women never had time to ponder upon their limitations and curses. Their GRATITUDE feeling attracted great positive achievements in their life. They used kindness as the weapon to win hearts and followed their passion irrespective of credit given by the society to lead a happier life.

Dr. Aditi Pant is the first Indian woman oceanographer to visit the frozen Antarctica for Indian Antarctica Program. She has held several key positions at various institutions including the National

Institute of Oceanography, National Chemical Laboratory, University of Pune, and Maharashtra Academy of Sciences.

She was born in Nagpur in a poor family. She got scholarship from US government to do her master's degree in Marine Sciences in the University of Hawaii. Post that she then pursued her PhD in Physiology on Marine Algae in London University. She then returned to India and joined National Institute of Oceanography in Goa focusing on coastal studies.

In 1983, along with the structural geologist Sudipta Sengupta, Aditi became the first Indian women to join the third expedition to step into the Antarctic region. This expedition aimed at researching on food chain physics, chemistry, and biology in the Antarctic Ocean. The team has built the first Indian scientific research base station of Antarctica.

She holds five patents and many publications in International journals. She was honoured with the Antarctica Award by the Government of India.

She is a great example that women can not only reach space but can also travel to the farthest untouched regions on earth and into the ocean. Awards or fame has never been an important milestone for these game changers. Their personal sense of achievement and happiness is what matters for them the most in life.

Optimism is the faith that leads to achievement.
Nothing can be done without hope and confidence.
– Helen Keller

Women are known for breaking barriers. Neighbours, relatives, friends and sometimes even your own family members might tend to ignore and criticize you. But do not give room to allow their criticism bother you. Instead focus on your goals, work hard and let your success be the best revenge against such criticisers.

These women never gave the authority to the bad situations or disparagers to demotivate them. Instead of letting their critics to de-energize themselves, their OPTIMISTIC outlook helped them to rise above it. They never allowed the external things to decide their happiness level. They knew that happiness starts from within, in our thoughts, and in the PRESENT moment, not in the future. They realized that the sense of ACHIEVEMENT is important to lead a happy life.

Sathyasri Sharmila is the first transgender lawyer in India who has crossed the barriers with determination. She worked as an activist for their community.

She was born as Udhayakumar at Ramanathapuram district in Tamil Nadu. She stepped out of her home at the age of 18 as her neighbours insulted and ill-treated her. She then changed her name and completed B.Com in Company Secretaryship. Later, to serve the LGBTQ community, she shifted her focus to the field of law and completed Bachelors of Law in 2007.

Sharmila waited for a decade, and only in 2018, she registered her name with Bar Council of Tamil Nadu and Puducherry. In an interview, she said that, "...as Supreme Court recognized transgender to be registered as third gender and situation started gradually improving, I came forward to register my name as a lawyer. I wanted to serve my community..."

She had to face many struggles and discouragement throughout her life to achieve this position. She reminds me of Eckhart Tolle's beautiful saying, *"The primary cause of unhappiness is never the situation but your thoughts about it."* She conquered her fears and learnt the secret of happy living.

Though it took a decade for her to develop courage to register her name in the State Bar Council, the moment she did, she realized the real worth of crossing all her troubles and obstacles she faced in her life. She is a great inspiration for many youngsters to knock off all the barriers and take a courageous step to move forward to pursue one's passion.

We can complain because rose bushes have thorns or rejoice because thorn bushes have roses.

*— **Abraham Lincoln***

These women were highly OPTIMISTIC in nature. They always looked at everything with a positive outlook - 'glass half full' attitude. But at the same time, they learnt to accept the reality and knew their weaknesses that required attention. They learnt to act on those weaknesses without being embarrassed. They worked hard for many years, with enthusiasm and optimistic thoughts, not to get fame or materialistic wealth but to feel the sense of ACHIEVEMENT at their heart. Their optimistic thoughts and strong focus on their end goal helped them to overcome their fears and become a role-model for youngsters of India.

Saina Nehwal is an Indian professional badminton player who has won about 25 International titles. She has represented India three times in Olympics and won a bronze medal in 2012, becoming the first Indian badminton player to win an Olympics medal. She is the first Indian to win a Super Series title.

She was born in Hisar, Haryana, and grew up in Hyderabad, Telangana. When she was born, her grandmother refused to see her for a month because she was a girl – a form of discrimination prevalent in many parts of rural India. But now, Saina is the brand ambassador of Haryana.

Her first of many badminton victories happened when she won the Junior National Championship at the age of 13. She created a huge impact by winning two singles gold medals in Commonwealth Games. She had won back to back in 5 International tournaments, both in the year 2010 and 2012.

However, her journey to success was not without struggles. She suffered several major injuries but her positivity and self-confidence helped her to recover from them quickly. Initially, her parents had to borrow money, from friends and relatives, to manage Saina's training expenses. Neither her early financial struggles nor injuries de-motivated her from becoming a champion.

In 2015, her dream came true when she became the first Indian women player to hold world's number 1 rank in badminton. She won maiden women's singles title at the India Open BWF Super Series which made her to top in the Badminton World Federation (BWF) world rankings. She became the highest paid badminton player in the world. She was honoured with the sporting awards - Arjuna and Rajiv Gandhi Khel Ratna. She was also conferred the Padma Shri and the Padma Bhushan.

Saina's optimistic attitude and her authentic happiness goal helped her to achieve the highest victories.

Optimism is a happiness magnet. If you stay positive, good things and good people will be drawn to you.
— Mary Lou Retton

If you observe these women, they had to face many struggles in their life. But they never perceived them as show stoppers rather used them as stepping stones to achieve their dream. They learnt many things from their role models and coach but believed they had the potential to surpass them. They knew how to bring true happiness into their lives. Also, many women realized the real HAPPINESS in them, when they started having selfless thoughts for the benefit of the community at large.

On this fifth night of Navaratri, I want you to think about these qualities to become a vibrant woman. You need to understand that your happiness level depends on the value of your positive thoughts. So, BELIEVE in yourself and believe you will be successful in achieving your goal in the near future. I want you to incubate YELLOW colour qualities within yourself. Be kind, optimistic and do the work that gives you real happiness.

Those who are happiest are those who do the most for others.
– Booker T. Washington

The audio stopped.

That day, I learned how we ourselves are responsible to bring happiness into our lives. Without knowing this, we end up searching for happiness everywhere around the world. I realized how to lead a happy life. The love these women must have had to achieve their passion and their sacrifices to make it a possibility made me realize the real power of a woman.

The next morning, I woke up stronger than ever before, with clarity on what my life purpose is, that which will promise me authentic happiness in my life. I streamlined my thoughts and decided to take determined steps to meet my goal of becoming a world renowned scientist.

I spend the entire morning with my grandmother helping her make garlands and in other preparation work for the pooja. During lunch, my grandfather advised me, "You should carry a fearless attitude to face failures in life like your mother, Shivani." I knew he is very proud of my mother. He then shared the story about how he had to spend 30 years to legally sort out a property dispute. A close relative of ours betrayed him and seized all his farms. As my grandfather had the legal documents showing the land deeds in his name, he filed a case in court trusting our judicial system for justice. He had to take care of 3 children with no income till he got back his lands. On top of it, he had to cope with the lawyer fees and other legal expenses for 3 decades to get justice.

I was dismayed that our laws are not stringent to protect people, and honest citizens waste many years to receive justice. As the judicial system forms the backbone of a country, the gaps in the law don't seem to have been addressed in spite of such problems faced by the common men. I wondered why has our government not taken measure to close every legal appeal within a stipulated period for timely closure of all legal cases!?

After finishing the evening pooja at our home, we headed to the Durga temple.

Chapter 7

Growth, Health and Harmony

" Nature always wears the colours of the spirit."

-   **Ralph Waldo Emerson**

" The sixth day of Navaratri is dedicated to goddess Katyayani, an avatar of Durga. She took birth as the daughter of sage Katyayan to end evil forces. She is also known as 'Mahishasura Mardini' as she destroyed the demon, Mahishasura who troubled the gods. To prepare herself for the war, the goddess armed herself with the divine weapons, received from other Gods, like trident, vajra, mace, bent sword, bow, axe and shield. She is portrayed as emitting bright light from her body to kill darkness and evil forces. She is depicted with a fearsome sight – with anger and wild hair, eighteen arms holding various weapons and riding a magnificent lion. Those who pray her with utmost faith will be blessed with growth and good health. She removes diseases, sorrows and guilt from her devotees for their well-being and harmony in life," said grandma.

When we entered the temple, I was astonished at the beautiful decoration of goddess Durga in a posture of killing the demon. I sensed the pleasant energy charge in the surrounding environment. The mesmerising floral decoration and pleasant smile on the goddess' statue reminded me of my mother's words about the 'Law of Universal Oneness.' According to this law, everything in this world is CONNECTED to a single source that makes up this Universe. Every living being and every non-living things are made up of energy and this ENERGY governs the movement of everything in the Universe.

As I was gifted with green attire that day, I knew that my mother would share the qualities of green colour that day. When I entered my room, I noticed a small gift parcel on the bed along with a handwritten note, "Do you have GREEN colour traits? It's time to explore within you. Act now." I opened the gift and it was a pleasing green crystal which had the inscription - ***"Growth, Health and Harmony"***.

I received the audio message from my mother. I tapped on the message.

GREEN is the colour of GROWTH and HARMONY. It is regarded as the creative power of the Universe and colour of the nature. This green crystal represents the traits like unconditional love towards environment, natural health, stability, growth, freshness, harmony and fertility. Green represents personal development and new beginnings in life.

Strength and growth come only through
continuous effort and struggle.
– Napoleon Hill

Generally, these women evoke a sense of growth, fertility, peace and serenity. They continuously strive to improve themselves and quickly adapt to changes around them. They carry fresh and unique ideas. They are admired for their individuality.

HEALTH is the most important and greatest wealth of mankind. Being healthy is about taking care of our body, by eating good healthy food, and mind, by giving importance to our desires to pursue our passion. Hence, being healthy refers to taking good care of both our physical and mental being. Only after we are healthy, we can start working to safeguard our nature and environment.

Due to the importance given on earning materialistic wealth, many of us end up being too busy in the rat race and forget to give importance to a healthy diet. Though it might seem simple, it's not so easy to change our diet. It requires determination to switch to healthy food habits. Jean Anthelme Brillat-Savarin beautifully said, *"Tell me what you eat and I will tell you who you are."*

Sunitha Narain, a well-known environmental activist, writer and social worker is the Director General of research institute, the Centre for Science and Environment (CSE). She is also the editor of the *'Down to Earth'* magazine. She plays a vital role in environmental policy formulation and development in India. She was a member of the Indian Prime Minister's Council on Climate Change.

She was born in Delhi. She was awarded with a Honorary Doctorate in Science by the University of Calcutta.

In 1980, after her studies, she started her work as a co-researcher with the founder of CSE, Anil Agarwal, an eminent and committed environmentalist. She researched on the environmental issues and sustainable development and took several initiatives to manage the environment. She co-authored, with Anil Agarwal, in their publication, *'Towards Green Villages'* on the subject of local democracy and sustainable development. She co-edited the State of India's Environment report. She has authored many publications on environmental development, water supply related issues and pollution.

In 1991, she co-authored *'Global warming in an unequal world: A case of environmental colonialism,'* which played a critical role in establishing the principle of equity on climate change. In 2012, she had authored the 7th State of India's Environment Reports, Excreta Matters, which presents a comprehensive analysis of urban India's water and pollution challenges.

In 2005, the CSE, under her leadership was awarded with the Stockholm Water Prize. She was honoured with the Padma Shri by the Government of India for her contributions to the environmental science. She was listed among the list of *100 Most Influential People* by Time Magazine in 2016. She also received the World Water Prize for her work on rainwater harvesting.

Harmony is a beautiful balance between mind, body and soul measured in tender peaceful moments.
— Melanie Koulouris

These women realized the importance of being HEALTHY to achieve their vision. With healthy mind and healthy body, they had HARMONY in life. They knew that maintaining good health by adopting good eating habits is the basic foundation to pursue our dreams.

For these women, GROWTH is nothing but a consistent effort to improve themselves. They knew that we ourselves are the best competent for us and NOT others. They focused on their daily improvement by comparing themselves to the previous day. They weren't afraid of failures but were afraid of quitting and made daily progress at least baby steps. Their LEARNING ATTITUDE to come out of their comfort zone and get adapted to the new environment helped them to grow continuously. In fact, they considered some of their life struggles are good and healthy because without them they would not be as strong as they are now.

Mary Kom, an Indian Olympic boxer is the only boxer to win eight World Championship medals. She has won seven gold medals in various boxing championships. This got her the nick name, *'Magnificent Mary'*.

She became the first Indian woman boxer to win a Gold Medal in the Asian Games in 2014 and in 2018 Commonwealth Games. She is the only woman to become World Amateur Boxing Champion for six times. She had also been ranked as number 1 in International Boxing Association (AIBA) World Women's Ranking Light Flyweight category.

She was born in a village at Churachandpur district of Manipur to poor parents. During her school days, Mary wasn't good in her studies but had interest in athletics. She got inspired by the Indian boxer Dingko Singh, a fellow Manipuri who won a gold medal in 1998 Bangkok Asian Games. Mary left her hometown to study at the state academy in Imphal when she was fifteen. That decision created a turning point in her life. She became a great example that not everyone needs to be good in studies as long as they understand their interest and pursue their passion.

She has three sons - twins born in 2007 and another son in 2013. Despite her personal family commitments, she continuously won several championships throughout her career. She smartly managed to balance her personal life, and career and became the best example for accomplishing all the responsibilities of a women. The process of giving birth is considered as an emotional roller-coaster ride by many working women. But if you observe, every successful woman has learnt to balance personal and professional life because for them both are equally important and they never compromise one for the other. That is the speciality of a winning woman.

She has received various honours from Indian Government including Arjuna award, Rajiv Gandhi Khel Ratna award, Padma Shri and Padma Bhushan.

I believe that the greatest gift you can give your family and the world is a healthy you.
— Joyce Meyer

There are women pioneers who didn't stop with just taking care of their family. They came forward to support a bigger cause, to protect nature. Being a woman, CARING attitude comes naturally to them. They understand the need to protect the nature, irrespective of governmental support. They worked hard with passion to save mountains and spread their passion among public to create greener planet.

Dr. Harshwanti Bisht, a mountaineer, Economics professor and Himalaya saver contributed to ecological conservation in the mountainous region of Gangotri area in Uttarakhand. During the last 25 years, her *Save Gangotri* project has planted several thousands of saplings, propagated threatened medicinal herbs, organized eco-awareness programs and educated travellers about the need for responsible tourism.

She is from Dehradun. She got inspired to work in Gangotri when she saw the great effect of Edmund Hillary's work to conserve the natural environment and to bring economic opportunities to the Sherpa communities.

In 1981, Harshwanti along with Rekha Sharma, and Chandra Prabha Aitwal were the first three women to summit the main peak of Nanda Devi. She was also a member of the Indian expedition to Mt. Everest in 1984. She worked in restoring the birch forests around the terminal area of Gangotri glacier, in her attempt to stabilise the receding glacier at the headwaters of the river Ganga.

She urges that women need to develop a habit of finding opportunity in every difficulty they face. And treat it as a chance to improve the lives of individuals, communities, and in turn the whole planet. Through her project, *Mountain Power*, she aims to setup a network of women mountaineering clubs throughout Himalayan region to conserve nature and to protect the legacy of mountains.

She was honoured with the Sir Edmund Hillary Mountain Legacy Medal. This award recognizes patrons with similar drive as Sir Hillary's lifelong commitment to the welfare of mountain people and the environment.

He who lives in harmony with himself lives in harmony with the Universe.
– Marcus Aurelius

Not many women get the support and encouragement from family to pursue their passion in sports. Many think that women in sports have to compromise on many things in their personal life. But there are wonder women who are smart enough to create a happy family and brave enough to work hard CONSISTENTLY to chase their dreams. Their parents and/or spouse were ready to compromise little things in the interest of seeing their daughter/wife as a champion. With the support of their family, these women cultivated never-settle-for-less attitude in life. Parental support and personal sacrifices with strong focus on growth has created a world weightlifting champion.

Saikhom Mirabai Chanu is an Indian weightlifter who has won gold medal in the World Weightlifting Championships during the year

2017. She has won multiple medals in Commonwealth Games in the 48kg category.

She was born in Imphal, Manipur. She hails from a poor family and her parents identified her physical strength at the age of twelve. Her informal weightlifting training started, by carrying firewood blocks to her home for cooking. She gave importance to her personal growth though she couldn't afford formal trainings due to her family situation. Though weightlifting sport requires having a healthy nutritious diet - she couldn't afford it during the initial days. But later a Mumbai based textile company helped her financially to become a champion.

She was trained by one of the popular weightlifting sportswomen and Indian national coach, Kunjarani Devi. Her first breakthrough came in at Glasgow Commonwealth Games in 2014 where she won a silver medal and bagged a gold medal again in 2018. In 2016, she broke the 12-year national record of her coach in 2016 Olympics trails in Patiala.

She lifted a total of 201 kilograms at 2019 World Weightlifting Championships to finish 4th and created a new national record in the 49Kg category. She also won in several other championships.

She is the recipient of India's highest civilian sports honour, Rajiv Gandhi Khel Ratna award. She was also honoured with the Padma Shri in 2018.

Some struggle is healthy. If you can embrace it rather than be angry, you can use it as your pilot light.
— Damon Wayans

India has a pioneer business woman in healthcare field who worked hard to raise the bar of clinical health care practices across the country. Irrespective of economic fluctuations, health industry plays an important role to protect and safe-guard people towards living a HEALTHY life. Mahatma Gandhiji beautifully said, *"It is health that is real wealth and not pieces of gold and silver."*

Dr. Preetha Reddy is the vice chairperson of Apollo Hospitals, one of the largest Indian healthcare conglomerates. With guidance from her father, Dr. Prathap C Reddy, she joined Apollo hospitals as the Joint Managing Director in 1989. Till then, she worked in an advertising agency and was a full time mother for her sons.

Five years later, she became the Managing Director of Apollo hospitals. She worked with government and several private companies to bring good improvements in the healthcare policies. In 2014, she became the executive vice-chairperson of Apollo hospitals. She worked hard to enhance the hospital facilities and bring in several quality standards to patients. She procured state of art equipment and hired best talents across all the branches.

Keeping with the wishes of her father, Preetha ensures the guiding principle of Apollo is to *"provide the best health care to the maximum number of patients through tender loving care at the lowest possible cost."*

Started as a 150-bed hospital in Chennai in 1983 by Dr. Prathap C Reddy, now Apollo Hospitals is one of the largest healthcare providers in Asia, with over 8000 beds across 46 hospitals in India and abroad. Since its inception, Apollo has touched the lives of over 120 million individuals across 140 countries. She was also elected to the board of medical technology company, Medtronic as an independent director.

She holds a master's degree in Public Administration. Later, she was conferred the Doctor of Science degree by Dr M.G.R. Medical

University for her outstanding contribution and dedication in the field of healthcare.

She launched *'Save A Child's Heart Initiative' (SACHi)* that provides cardiac care to the underprivileged children with congenital heart diseases. She is also responsible for the development of Apollo's Isha Vidya Rural School that focuses on supporting underprivileged children from rural areas. She formed the National Quality Council, a body that provides guidelines and quality standards to Indian hospitals and nursing homes.

In the book, *30 Women In Power,* she says, *"Women have to juggle the family at home and the family at work. My passion towards profession never made me to compromise on the time we spend with our family at home. The question of choosing one over the other never arises as each has its own importance and its own role."*

Considering her contribution to the healthcare sector, Dr. Preetha has been featured in the International list of *50 Most Powerful Women in Business*, compiled by Fortune, for three consecutive years – 2009, 2010, and 2011.

Dr. Prathap feels that Apollo's success is due to the education and empowerment of his four daughters. It's he who taught them since their childhood to face adversity with courage and not to be overwhelmed by fear. He says, *"Women have capability and skill, but they don't get opportunity to demonstrate it, which my daughters had and they have done extremely well."*

This woman demonstrated that best education provided to children without any gender discrimination has led to a huge win for the healthcare conglomerate.

*Always aim at complete harmony of thought
and word and deed. Always aim at purifying
your thoughts and everything will be well.*
– Mahatma Gandhi

On this sixth night of Navaratri, I want you to think about these qualities to become a vibrant woman. You need to understand that your happiness is the result of good health and conscience. By making your body more efficient, you can achieve your goals efficiently. Having HEALTHY MIND and HEALTHY BODY is your best investment for leading your extra-ordinary life. Winston Churchill beautifully said, *"Healthy citizens are the greatest asset any country can have"*. I want you to incubate GREEN colour qualities within yourself. Be healthy, focus on your growth always and aim for harmony in your life.

*Those who contemplate the beauty of the earth
find reserves of strength that will endure as long
as life lasts.*
– Rachel Carson

The audio stopped.

That day, I understood the importance of health and harmony. I realized how women smartly manage their time for the welfare of their self, their family and the society, making India proud of them. I understood they are the real gems of India. And it dawned on me, why mom gifted me different colour CRYSTALS to portray the qualities of Indian wonder women.

The next morning, I woke up feeling blessed to be born as a woman. I spend that day helping my grandmother in the pooja preparations.

At noon, while we were arranging the idols, my friend, Meena and her cousin came home. Meena is a close friend and our neighbour. She was also visiting her grandparents for semester holidays. Meena, Ajay and I used to play a lot as kids, as we all usually spend every summer vacation in our home town. Meena is in final year of bachelor's degree in Commerce at Loyola College, Chennai; whereas her cousin Isha is studying Fashion Designing from the same college.

I was meeting Isha for the first time. After quick introductions, we started talking about our old memories - how Meena and I used to roam around our mango farm and one time we were bitten by honey bees while playing in the farm.

Then the conversation shifted to our college experiences. I was puzzled by Isha's attitude towards her fellow college grads. She looked modern and beautiful but I felt her thoughts were superfluous and self-centred. She seemed to give lot of importance to her dressing style. She seemed money minded and lacked compassion towards others. She spoke about her boyfriends and how she took advantage of them to finish her assignments, fulfilling her shopping needs, or canteen expenses, etc. Meena and I felt weird at some of her experiences though we did not openly express our feelings towards her.

After they left in couple of hours, my grandmother asked me, "Don't you feel something is wrong with Isha?"

I couldn't hide my feelings anymore and openly commented on her attire and her opinion about boys. Despite the fact that she is currently in a village, she didn't know how to choose right attire while attending Navaratri celebration. Infact, my grandmother was upset, as she thought Isha visited our home in her swim suit. That day, I realized the importance of parenting as I started comparing Meena and Isha. Both are from well off family, have educated parents, are exposed to city life style and study in the same college. But there seems to be a huge difference in their thoughts and moral values. This incident instilled in me the real need for educating the women as they also unknowingly contribute to crimes against women.

After finishing the evening pooja at our home, we headed to the Durga temple.

Chapter 8

Authority, Maturity and Neutrality

" The purest and most thoughtful minds are those which love colour the most."

-   John Ruskin

" **T**he seventh manifestation of Durga is goddess Kalaratri, which means, *'one who destroys darkness or ends ignorance.'* She is portrayed as the destroyer of evil, the fiercest and most fearsome deity with dark complexion, wild hair, four hands, three protruding red eyes, and tongue, seated on a donkey. She is also referred to as 'Kali matha.' Kali was created to kill two demons – Shumbha and Nishumbha, who defeated Lord Indra. They send another demon, Raktabija to battle with Kali. He had a boon that every drop of his blood that would fall on the ground would create a clone of him. Realizing this, Kali killed Raktabija and drank all his blood preventing from dropping on the ground. She then killed Shumbha and Nishumbha and got back the lost kingdom of other gods. She holds vajra and dagger to fight against evil forces and negative energies. She destroys darkness of worry from lives of her devotees and makes them fearless. She offers authority and several other leadership qualities to those who worship her," said grandma.

I had a surprise at the temple. That day, the decoration of the goddess Durga was very unique. Though the statue was decorated to appear angry with a frightening look, since I understood the meaning of this avatar from my grandmother, the terrifying look didn't bother me.

As I was gifted with grey attire that day, I knew that my mother would share the qualities of grey colour. I quickly finished dinner and stepped into my room looking for the daily gift. I noticed a small gift parcel on the bed along with a handwritten note, "Do you have GREY colour traits? It's time to explore within you. Act now." I opened the gift and it was an alluring grey crystal which had the inscription - *"Authority, Maturity and Neutrality"*.

I tapped on the audio message received from my mother.

GREY is the colour of NEUTRALITY and PROTECTION. This grey crystal represents the strength of transformation, balances the energy and keeps people down to earth. Many a time women need to take unemotional and unbiased decisions in their role and act maturely. Their authority demands them to be neutral and stable decision maker. Grey colour traits will help you to use your authority rightly and meet your responsibilities.

Authority without wisdom is like a heavy axe
without an edge, fitter to bruise than polish.
- Anne Bradstreet

Generally, these women have balanced emotions, unbiased nature, are very practical and highly mature, and possess authority with calmness, self-sufficiency and intelligence. Grey colour personalities are usually known for their practical and futuristic thoughts, intelligence, neutrality and stability.

AUTHORITY is different from power. Power is applied by forcing others to obey your commands whereas authority, in contrast, is the right to give command, obeyed by others. Legitimate power is often called as authority. It possesses 2 key characteristics - accountability and rationality. Often, this trait is highly visible in entrepreneurs and business executives. These women have power, control and respect for others which makes them highly successful in meeting their vision. They know what they want to achieve, and they keep up their words.

Gita Gopinath, an Indian-American economist is the Chief Economist of the International Monetary Fund (IMF). International Finance and Macroeconomics are her favourite area of research.

She is the John Zwaanstra Professor of International Studies and Economics at Harvard University. She is the Co-Director of the International Finance and Macroeconomics program at the National Bureau of Economic Research. During 2016 to 2018, she was the Economic Adviser to the Chief Minister of Kerala. She is a visiting scholar at the Federal Reserve Bank of Boston, a member of the economic advisory panel of the Federal Reserve Bank of New York and co-editor of the 2019 edition of the Handbook of International Economics.

She was born in Kolkata, and received her master's degree in Economics from Delhi School of Economics and in University of Washington. In 2001, she received her PhD degree at Princeton University. She was awarded with the Princeton's Woodrow Wilson Fellowship Research Award while doing her doctoral research. She has authored many articles on exchange rates, international financial crises, monetary policy, trade and investment policies and emerging market crises.

In 2011, she was chosen as a Young Global Leader (YGL) by the World Economic Forum. She was awarded with the Pravasi Bharatiya Samman, the highest honour conferred on overseas Indians. In 2014, she was named one among *The Top 25 economists under 45* by the IMF.

She is one of the best examples of a highly knowledgeable and qualified economist known for her intelligence.

Authority doesn't come from the loudest voice,
but the wisest.
- J.R. Morales

As leaders often say, MATURITY is not measured by age, but is realized by one's actions and decisions. Matured women are known for self-awareness, humility, open-mindedness and compassion. By nature, they live by values and they are emotionally STRONG, unshaken equally by praise or criticism. They tend to express gratitude for every small thing they possess in life. They tend to prioritize others' needs over their personal desires. Despite their wisdom, they always tend to seek experienced people's opinion without assuming they have all the answers.

Nirupama Menon Rao, a retired Foreign Secretary and Ambassador served as India's Foreign Secretary from 2009 to 2011. Then she took over her role as India's Ambassador to the United States where she served for a term of two years from 2011 to 2013.

She was born in Malappuram, Kerala and hails from an army family. In 1973, she topped the All India Civil Services Examination for both the Indian Foreign Services and the Indian Administrative Services.

She carries four decades of experience in her career. She is India's first woman spokesperson in the Ministry of External Affairs, New Delhi. She also served as India's first women Ambassador to China and high commissioner to Sri Lanka.

As a diplomat, she has travelled around the world and served at South America, Asia, Europe, and the United States. She said that her mother had powerful influence on her and she feels that women could bring something very special to a profession like diplomacy because of the ability to think in a 360-degree manner with inclusivity in mind. She lived by Sir Albert Einstein's words, *"Blind belief in authority is the greatest enemy of truth."*

She served as a Fellow at the Weatherhead Centre for International Affairs at Harvard University where she got specialized on Asia-Pacific Security. She holds the Honorary Doctorate of Letters from Pondicherry University. She is the recipient of many awards including Vanitha Rathnam Award and the Kalinga Karubaki Literary Award to name a few.

She runs a trust, the South Asian Symphony Foundation that aims to improve the cause of peace and mutual understanding in South Asia through the medium of music. In 2018, Rao received the Fellowship of Peace Award conferred by the Mahatma Gandhi Memorial Centre, Washington D.C.

As always a woman's success isn't without sacrifices. Dr. Nirupama married an IAS officer, Sudhakar Rao who was the Chief Secretary of Karnataka. Her job required continuous hectic travel across countries, whereas her husband's job was in the state of Karnataka. But they had great understanding and sense of mutual commitments. They agreed to live separately and catch up with family only during holidays. Despite compromising on living a conventional married life, both trusted on each other. Their children also had to adjust to this lifestyle, for the sake of their parents' strong commitment to serve the country.

*One of the truest signs of maturity is the
ability to disagree with someone while still
remaining respectful.*
- Dave Willis

RESILIENCY is one of the powerful traits of these women. They knew how to strengthen themselves from negative experiences. They always account to influence others without taking advantage of their power. They often react to emotional situations with EQUANIMITY. They love to collaborate with others and ask for help without their ego getting in their way. These women remind me of Roy T. Bennett's saying, *"Maturity is when you stop complaining and making excuses and start making changes."* They always explore ways to improve and grow by being supportive of others.

Ritu Kapur is an Indian media entrepreneur who is the Co-Founder and CEO of Quintillion Media, a digital media company. She also Co-Founded 'The Quint', a web based digital news site with her husband. She is also one of the founding members of Network18.

Within 3 years, her digital news platform witnessed 100% growth and marked its presence among India's mainstream news websites. She is also a strategic investor in other digital media platforms such as The News Minute, SHEROS and Youth Ki Awaaz. She is an advisory board member in the Reuters Institute for the Study of Journalism (RISJ).

She holds a master's degree in Film and TV Production. She produced *THE INDIA SHOW*, the first local production show on Star Plus satellite channel. In 1995, she started directing and writing screenplays for television shows. Her drama series, *Bhanwar* won the *Best Investigative Series* at Videocon-Screen Awards. Ritu was both director and screenplay writer on the series that ran on Sony Entertainment Channel.

In 2008, she pioneered Citizen Journalism (CJ) on Indian Television when she launched *The CJ* show on CNN IBN which later won numerous awards. The platform enabled many Indians to contribute and raise the issues faced by people around them by using their mobile phones, as a news sharing enabler.

In 2011, she launched History TV18, a joint venture with A+E Networks. She took the role as Head of Programming while continuing in CNN IBN as the Features Editor. There she produced *The Greatest Indian* poll that generated more than 20 million online votes. In 2014 general election, she launched several campaigns to educate and create awareness among Indians about their voter rights.

She is also an advisory board member at the British Council for their Future News Worldwide partnership program. She is also a board member of the World Editor's Forum.

True Leadership is the authority given by the trust of the followers to use power for the benefit of all.
- **Myles Munroe**

These women are known for respecting others' point of views and beliefs. They are brave enough to identify what doesn't work. They take CONSISTENT effort to bring different actions to make it working. They are straight-forward, and stand-up for fairness without any bias. They listen to others more and talk less, which helps them make right decisions without being inconsiderate towards anyone.

Naina Lal Kidwai, an Indian banker and business executive was the former Group General Manager and CEO of HSBC India. She was also the former president of the Federation of Indian Chambers of Commerce and Industry.

Born in Delhi, she holds bachelor's degree in Economics from Delhi University and master's degree in Business Administration from Harvard Business School. She is the first Indian women to graduate from Harvard. She is also a charted accountant.

She started her banking career at ANZ Grindlays. She then served as the Head of Investment Banking in Morgan Stanley, India. And then, she moved to Standard Chartered Bank, where she was the Chief Manager of Retail Bank and Investment Bank.

Currently, she is the Chairman of HSBC Asset Management Pvt Ltd and HSBC InvestDirect Securitites Pvt Ltd at India. Along with serving as the Chairman of Max Financial Services Ltd. She is also a non-executive director on the board of Nestle, Chairwoman at City of London's India Advisory Council, and Global Advisor at Harvard Business School, among others.

Hailing from a family of achievers, she is a self-motivated and a confident woman known for negotiation skills. She has developed exceptional investment strategies for leading banks and IT firms. She supports several community organizations such as India's Self-Employed Women's Association and Digital Partners, a non-profit organization managed by her husband dedicated to closing the technology gap between rich and poor.

Naina has received many national and International honours. She was one among the *25 Most Powerful Women in Indian Business* by Business *Today.* She is the recipient of Padma Shri award for her contributions in banking, trade and finance sector.

Maturity is not when we start speaking big things. It is when we start understanding small things.
- **Author Unknown**

Highly responsible and accountable in all situations of life is an important attribute of these women. They assess themselves by taking a neutral stance to watch their thoughts and actions before taking decisions. They tend to be NEUTRAL and their unbiased decision making skill helps them to achieve big things in life. Without mental barriers, they are OPEN to ideas and opinions maintaining a positive attitude. As these women are highly matured, they ANALYSE the situation of the person who tries to bring them down instead of meting out for their wrong behaviour.

Kiran Mazumdar, one of the top women entrepreneurs of India is the Chairperson and Managing Director of Bengaluru based biotechnology company, Biocon Limited. She was also the Chairperson of Indian Institute of Management, Bengaluru.

Born in Bengaluru, she graduated in Zoology from Bangalore University. She then earned her master's degree in Brewing at Ballarat College, Melbourne University at her father's suggestion. She later received honorary doctorate from Indian and several foreign universities based on her contribution in the field of biotechnology. She started her professional career working as a trainee brewer and as a trainee maltster at Australia. After four years, she started working at Biocon Biochemicals Limited in Ireland, which gave her the opportunity to start Biocon Indian subsidiary.

Having started the company with a small initial investment in her garage, she had several setbacks to raise fund to expand her business in India. But she never got disappointed due to lack of support and never stopped chasing her passion. Rather, she worked harder. With determination, she built one of the leading biotech companies in India. Under the supervision and leadership of this sixty seven years old business woman, Biocon has evolved from an enzymes manufacturing company to fully-integrated bio-pharmaceutical company with various business portfolio products - focussing on diabetes, oncology and other auto-immune diseases.

Kiran's thought leadership, ideas on business expansion plans and her continuous focus on innovation and research became the backbone of Biocon. Biocon has filed about 950 patent applications, based on its research activity. In the year 2004, Biocon became the first biotechnology company of India to issue an IPO. Biocon became the second Indian company to cross the market value of 1 billion dollars mark on the very first day.

Her Biocon Foundation focuses on health, education and infrastructure in rural areas of Karnataka that lack healthcare facilities. She established a non-profit organization, Mazumdar-Shaw Medical Foundation with a goal to create world class cancer centre. She is also part of the Bangalore City Connect Foundation, a non-profit trust for discussion of civic issues, involving both urban stakeholders and the government.

She is the recipient of several International awards including the Othmer Gold Medal for her outstanding contribution to science and chemistry, and Ernst & Young's Entrepreneur of the year award for Life Sciences and Healthcare. She is on the Financial Times' *Top 50 women in business list*. She is a global influencer and appeared on Forbes *2018 power women list*. She is the recipient of Indian civilian awards, the Padma Shri and Padma Bhushan.

Indeed, Kiran is one of the best examples of being a highly successful thought leader and a matured decision maker.

By staying neutral, I end up being somebody
that everybody can trust. Even if they don't
always agree with my decisions, they know I'm
not working against them.
- Linus Torvalds

On this seventh night of Navaratri, I want you to think about these qualities to become a vibrant woman. Always use your authority to take unbiased decisions by taking a neutral stand. You need to practice to be a responsible, stable and matured decision maker. Develop your emotional quotient, in order to take impartial decision for a given problem, without broadcasting your emotions. I want you to incubate GREY colour qualities within yourself. Work towards having Authority, Maturity and Neutrality in your life.

Maturity is learning to walk away from people and situations that threaten your peace of mind, self-respect, values, morals and self-worth.
- Buddha

The audio stopped.

That day, I understood the important qualities of LEADERSHIP personalities. I was under the assumption that grey represents dullness or dirtiness. I didn't realize the real meaning of being emotionally strong and neutral until mom clarified me, that day. I learned the management qualities represented by this colour.

The next morning, I woke up with a feeling of being a powerful woman. I spent the day helping my grandmother in the pooja preparations.

While cleaning the pooja room, I was collecting the floral waste on an old newspaper, which got my attention. It had news about the gang who sexually assaulted women for years in Pollachi district, Tamil Nadu. I quickly grabbed the paper and started reading it. I read that a gang of 7 to 8 men have sexually assaulted over 50 women in the past 7 years. The gang allegedly recorded videos of the assault and used them to blackmail the victims to gain money. Few women committed suicide as they were threatened with uploading their videos on the Internet and not many came forward to lodge the complaint against these criminals. The National Commission of Women (NCW) raised serious concern about women's safety and demanded detailed report after investigation was complete.

I was so concerned that these women were cheated due to their ignorance and weakness - not using social media for constructive purposes. I felt the need for parental support during such situation to safe guard every woman in their family. The criminals have betrayed women by exploiting their weakness. Parents need to educate their wards that betraying others is only a sin; getting betrayed is not a sin. I thought that every affected woman develop courage to learn the tough lesson from this incident and need to move on with normal life. They need to use social media carefully without unnecessarily revealing their personal details and avoid connecting with strangers.

After finishing the evening pooja at our home, we headed to the Durga temple.

Chapter 9

Care, Compassion and Hope

" Be uniquely you. Stand out. Shine. Be colourful. The world needs your prismatic soul."

- Amy Leigh Mercree

" The eighth day of Navaratri is dedicated to goddess Mahagauri, the most graceful avatar of goddess Durga. She is worshiped as the goddess of kindness and morality. After killing all the demons, goddess Kalaratri was teased for her dark skin by Lord Shiva. So, she prayed to Lord Brahma to get back her complexion. Brahma advised her to take bath in Mansarovar, a lake in Himalayas and finally she regains her fair skin. The name, 'Mahagauri' refers to a radiant beauty. She has four hands, wears white clothes, holds trident and tambourine in her hands and rides a white bull. It is believed that Mahagauri has great power to fulfil all our desires. The one who worships her will be relieved of sufferings in life and all the sins will get washed away. She blesses deep sense of inner-peace, hope, opulence, and life-long loving relationships to her devotees. She leads her devotees to a path of compassion and virtue," said grandma.

We spent about an hour in the temple and returned home with a peaceful mind, after hearing some interesting moral stories from my grandmother. As I was gifted with pink attire that day, I knew that my mother would share the qualities of pink colour that day.

I finished dinner and entered my room looking for the gift. I noticed a small gift parcel on the bed along with a handwritten note, "Do you have PINK colour traits? It's time to explore within you. Act now." I opened the gift and it was an astonishing pink crystal which had the inscription - ***"Care, Compassion and Hope"***.

I took my phone and typed the message, "Mom, the pink crystal looks more beautiful than all the other colour crystals that you have gifted me so far. May be all other crystals represents qualities to be developed for our own benefit, but only this crystal represents the qualities of being SELFLESS."

My mom replied with a smiley and said, 'Good, you are in a good form as I expected." And as the clock on my mobile showed 9 p.m., I received an audio message from her. I tapped on the message.

PINK is the colour of HOPE and COMPASSION. The pink colour crystal represents unconditional love, compassion and caring. It carries the power of red along with the calmness of white. This colour is associated with tenderness and nurturing qualities, and is a sign of hope. It also signifies the sweetness and innocence of a child living inside each of us. Pink colour traits will help you to live a fulfilling life as you learn to give back something to the people around you.

To make a difference in someone's life, you don't have to be brilliant, rich, beautiful, or perfect. You just have to care.
*- **Mandy Hale***

Generally, these women are calm, affectionate, insightful, and carry a mentoring attitude towards others. They carry a strong passion with gentle loving energy. These women are known for their unconditional love and care even towards unknown people.

Their COMPASSIONATE attitude makes these women receive more from almighty. Having selfless thoughts and caring about others' lives is also one of the most prevalent gestures of these women. They may not have been billionaires but they had a generous heart that helped them share whatever was available to them with others. Despite all struggles and darkness in their personal life, their CARING nature and HOPE to bring light in the lives of others, makes them to stand out in the crowd.

Aparna Lavakumar is a civil police officer at Irinjalakuda women's police station, Kerala and she is a mother of two. She hails from Amballur village near Thirissur city. Being a widow at a very young age, she raised both her daughters as a single parent.

She actively conducts awareness camps in schools and lectures on topics like law, traffic rules, and personal safety. In one of the camps, she met a bald boy of class five - a cancer survivor who lost his hair due to chemotherapy. The little boy got inspired from her speech and shared his dream to have a career in police department. This incident encouraged her to donate her hair to a non-profit organization, which prepares wigs for cancer survivors.

She says, *"Going bald can be severely traumatic for children with cancer, who are already battling for life at such a nascent age. I wanted to support them by proving that baldness is not a matter of shame."* Her brave act challenged the beauty standards and proved that feminine beauty does not lie in the physical looks but in purity of thoughts.

But that was not the first time, earlier she had cut off her hair partially to donate for a cause. About a decade earlier, in another incident, when the children of a homemaker where struggling to settle the hospital bill to get their mother's body released, without a second thought, she donated her gold bangles to release the dead body from a private hospital in Thrissur. Clearly, these selfless acts of this police officer are some of the best examples of love and compassion towards others.

A heart full of love and compassion is the main source of inner strength, will power, happiness and mental tranquillity.
- Dalai Lama

These women are those who realized that they were born with a great purpose - to take care of the society. Despite extreme difficulties and life-threatening situations in their personal life, they strive hard to HELP others overcome their difficulties. They remind me of the beautiful saying by Zayn Malik, *"No matter how hard life is. Don't lose hope."* These guardian angels have made our nation proud. They embody the real meaning for compassion.

Kousalya Periasamy was the first Indian women to bravely identify herself as an AIDS victim in the year 1995. Having lost her mother at the age of two, she grew up with her grandparents and stepmother. At the age of 19, she was forced to marry a close relative who was a lorry driver. Within few weeks after their marriage, she fell ill and was diagnosed HIV positive. Her husband died a few months later, and she was thrown out of the house, in spite of health problems. Though she was distressed and disappointed about her situation, she took a bold step and went public with her story. This not only changed her life but also put her on the forefront of a movement for a noble cause.

There wasn't much awareness about HIV during that time. Though she was scared initially, later she gained courage after consulting various women doctors. She was down with TB and meningitis in 1998. She had to manage huge medical expenses, as the drugs, though freely accessible now, weren't available in government hospitals during those days.

Despite all her struggles, in the same year, she with three other women founded a society called *Positive Women's Network* in Chennai to support the HIV victims. The society works hard to spread a simple message, *"Positive Living"*. That was a time when people believed in myths like the virus spreads through air or by touch. She believed that awareness about HIV will automatically create prevention measures. So, she worked hard to create awareness among patients and to support AIDS victims from humiliation. This four member network grew into more than 5000 strong network, with several units operating across all states in India.

The organization has worked with more than 30,000 HIV positive women in India. Through her organization, Kousalya wanted to teach the HIV positive women about their rights, as she believed that only when they are made aware about their rights, they can demand them. She fights to end the discrimination and humiliation meted to the HIV positive women in India. In an interview, she shared a shocking statistics, *"It is estimated that nearly 86 percent of the women got the virus from a single partner, in most cases their husband."*

From her personal experience, she guides HIV positive women to deal with daily challenges, and motivates them to share their experiences with other women in the society to create awareness about HIV.

In 2002, she organized the first National Consultation on women living with AIDS, transforming it into a national network. She got support from student volunteers and media to bring the public awareness. As per her request, *The Hindu* newspaper promised to provide a AIDS awareness article every month. She also conducts programs to stop discrimination among HIV positive children. In 2014, she was honoured with Nari Shakti Puraskar, which is the

Indian's highest civilian award for recognising the achievements and contributions of woman.

Compassion is to look beyond your own pain,
to see the pain of others.
- Yasmin Mogahed

The one who has hope has everything in their life. Hope forms the most essential trait of every woman who wants to live a fulfilling life. Hope forms the basis for a happy living. Talent, passion, optimism and ability helps but it's the HOPE which is the most basic pre-requisite and STIMULANT to achieve our goals. Amidst all struggles, it's was their hope and positive thoughts that became the torch to find their real life's purpose. Hope gave them the will and determination to pursue their goals. Hope gave them the courage to face inevitable challenges of life with a right mindset to SUCCEED in their vision.

Manasi Pradhan, an Indian women's rights activist and an author, is the founder of Honour for Women National Campaign, a movement that focuses on various activities to end violence against women in India. She is a member of the International Governing Council of World Women Organization. She founded a non-profit organization, OYSS Women, which organises women empowerment activities. The organization aims to help girl students for their higher education to develop them as future leaders in the society.

She was born in Khordha district, Odisha. From a young age, she was determined to complete her education. She graduated as the first women law graduate in her village. Despite strong pressure to stop her studies, her passion never gave room to be tired of walking 15 kilometres daily amidst hilly terrain to commute to her high school. She earned a bachelor's degree in Economics from

Government Women's College, Puri and master's degree in Odia literature from Utkal University. She then completed Bachelor's degree in Law.

She started her career working with the finance department, Government of Odisha and Andhra Bank. Later at the age of 21, she started her printing business and authored literary journals, which made her a successful entrepreneur.

She launched the Honour for Women National Campaign movement in the year 2009, which influenced the need to bring in serious amendments in the law against crimes towards women. The movement conducted various activities like women's rights festival, women's right literature, street shows, seminars and workshops to increase the awareness to fight against crimes. In 2014, she also founded Nirbhaya Vahini that released a four-point charter of demand, to all the state governments of India, emphasizing the need for women protection and to tackle violence against women.

In 2014, she was conferred with Rani Lakshmibai Stree Shakti Puraskar by the President of India. She had also won the *'Outstanding Women Award'* in 2011. In 2016, the New York based Bustle magazine named her among the *20 most inspiring feminists authors and activists.*

Let your hopes, not your hurts, shape your future.
- Robert H. Schuller

Sometimes life becomes a tragedy. There are many who live all or part of their life in self-pity and depression. They live wishing for death much before their actual death occurs. But despite trauma, stress and challenging situations, there are many women who DEDICATE their lives to fight for an important social cause, giving

MEANING to their life. They decided to own their destiny instead of giving antagonists the chance to decide their life. They believed their life purpose is to CARE for the society, irrespective of what society has done for them. They remind me of John F. Kennedy's beautiful words, *"Ask not what your country can do for you, ask what you can do for your country."*

Sunitha Krishnan is a social activist and co-founder of Prajwala, a non-governmental organization that rescues and offers rehabilitation support to victims of rape, women and children. She has published several books on these topics.

She was born in Bengaluru. She holds a master's degree in Social Work from Yenepoya University, Mangalore. From a young age, she had great interest to work for the society. She started teaching underprivileged children at the age of twelve. At the age of fifteen, while working on a campaign for Dalit community, she was gang raped by eight men for interfering in their society matters. She was beaten badly that left her partially deaf. Though she was shattered, this incident pushed her to work for the rape victims.

Though she didn't get her parents' support, she moved to Hyderabad to assist Brother Varghese Theckanath, a social activist who worked in People's Initiative Network for the betterment of people living in slums.

In 1996, she helped to evacuate the prostitutes in red light area in Hyderabad and provided them employment. She started a transition school, Prajwala, in the evacuated brothel to support the next generation children of these women. Later, this non-profit organization became a powerful network that focused on eradicating forced prostitution and sex trafficking. It has rescued about 12,000 prostitution victims and aided them in starting a new life. The organization provides moral, financial, legal and social support to the victims.

Prajwala is based on a five pillar strategic approach, namely – Prevention, Rescue, Rehabilitation, Reintegration and Advocacy. Many states have used clues from Sunitha's strategies to bring in similar rescue policies. In 2008, Prajwala won the prestigious AGFUND International Award for its revolutionary work to Combat Trafficking of Women and Children through Community Partnership. She was attacked and threatened many times but that didn't stop this brave heart to continue her selfless work.

In 2011, she was appointed as an advisor to draft the Government of Kerala's Nirbhaya Policy for Women and Children to fight against sexual violence. But later she resigned as she was not satisfied and in 2015, she got reappointed as Honorary Director in Nirbhaya scheme. She was also appointed as a member of the Andhra Pradesh State Women's Commission.

In 2016, she was honoured with Padma Shri and Nari Shakti Puraskar by Government of India. She is the recipient of several honours including Sri Sathya Sai Award for Human Excellence, Franco-German Award For Human Rights, and Mother Teresa award for Social Justice to name a few.

Compassion is the ultimate expression of your highest self.
- Russell Simmons

Their unconditional LOVE towards society differentiated them from the rest of the world. Knowing the importance of KINDNESS, they decided to gift their quality time to inspire others to live their best life. Their intelligence, passion and hope make them an example for divergent thinking. Beyond Intelligence Quotient (IQ) level, their positive attitude and fresh perspective makes them excellent problem solvers of social issues. They always had high self-efficacy, optimism and confidence to achieve their vision.

Lakshmi Menon is an eco-evangelist and social entrepreneur who runs *Pure Living*, an organization in Kerala that empowers elderly women and underprivileged people. The organization aims in creating eco-friendly solutions by growing a plant from disposed pens.

Lakshmi hails from Ernakulam district in Kerala. She is a designer by passion, completed her graduation in Home Science and worked in US as a jewellery designer for models in New York Fashion week.

She started *Pure Living* in 2012. With her designing skills and love for creating eco-friendly products, the idea to make seed – embedded disposable pens was born. These 'Pens with Love' are made from paper waste generated in printing press, and are embedded with seeds from Agastya tree – used in Ayurvedic medicines. The seeds grow into plants when the pen is disposed after usage, thus reducing plastic waste. *Pure Living* has sold over 1.5 lakh pens over the period of three years.

The enterprise also has a few other initiatives like manual lamp wicks and pencils rolled up from the recycled newspapers. The workers are usually senior citizens, orphans and differently-abled people contributing towards the national economy and green environment.

She was honoured as Earth Day Network Star by Earth Day Network Global in 2018. In the same year, she was selected as a governing council member of National Innovation Foundation.

The purpose of human life is to serve, and to show compassion and the will to help others.
- Albert Schweitzer

On this eighth night of Navaratri, I want you to think about these qualities to become a vibrant woman. SPIRITUAL AWARENESS is a source of compassion. Having concern for the welfare and well-being of others is a key trait to create meaning to our lives. Great spiritual leaders like Mahatma Gandhiji changed Indian history by their compassion. We need to VALUE people and experiences, over money. Believe that our knowledge will be wasted if it's not shared. Attract unconditional LOVE by showing unconditional love and care towards others. I want you to incubate PINK colour qualities within yourself. Be caring, compassionate and never lose hope at any point in life.

Only great souls know the grandeur there is
in charity.
- Jacques BeNigne Bossuet

The audio stopped.

That day, I learned the importance of cultivating selfless thoughts which would give us an ultimate sense of happiness. I was feeling proud of these women who worked for others' welfare sacrificing their own comfort and pleasure.

The next morning, I woke up with a strong feeling that I should give back something to the society for all the great things that I am blessed with in my life. I spent the day helping my grandmother in the preparation for pooja.

While we were arranging the idols, I couldn't stop myself from asking this question, "Grandma, why are women not bravely coming forward to talk about sexual harassment and to get legal punishment for the culprits?"

"Anila, there are few women who come forward to bring such incidents to light. But unfortunately, we do not have a safe platform yet where women can share her concerns openly. According to the government figures, there is an average of 92 rapes every day. But only a small percentage of women come forward to report their assault as there is no guarantee they will be heard and believed.

A few months earlier, a 23-year-old woman in Uttar Pradesh, a survivor of brutal rape by 5 men, was set on fire while she was on her way to the court for the hearing of her case. She suffered 80 percent burns and died in the hospital. This happened because the rapists were released on bail and attacked her with no fear of consequences. This clearly indicates the unavailability of a right platform for women to report against such crimes. Just a few months before this incident, a 26-year-old veterinary doctor at Hyderabad was gang raped. The rapists murdered her and dropped her corpse on the roadside.

Every day, I pray to Durga that the situation would change and Indian women get back the social status that she enjoyed during Vedic age. I am confident that my prayers will definitely be answered and am sure things will change soon. Mahatma Gandhiji said, *"The day a woman can walk freely on the roads at night, that day we can say that India has achieved independence."* I am sure I will see Independent India, before my death," said my grandma with tears in her eyes. I have never seen her shed tear before.

After completing the evening pooja at our home, we headed to the Durga temple.

Chapter 10

Creative, Grandeur and Wisdom

" Life is a sea of vibrant colour. Jump in."

— A.D. Posey

" **T**he ninth day of Navaratri is dedicated to the supreme goddess of power, Siddhidatri, the final avatar of Durga, who signifies perfection. The name refers to, 'giver of super natural power.' The ninth avatar is the embodiment of completeness and prosperity. All other forms of Durga are attributed with killing different demons, however, goddess Siddhidhatri manifested as a liberator. She embodies half of Lord Shiva, known by the name of Ardhanarishwar, symbolising the need for both masculinity and feminine energy for the creation of the Universe and every being in it. She bestowed eighteen super natural powers to Lord Shiva. The left half of the supreme power is a woman while the right half is a man. She is depicted as sitting on a fully bloomed lotus with a blissful smile on her face, riding a lion, and in her four hands carrying a chakra, mace, conch shell and lotus. She is the source of creativity. She guides devotees towards a disciplined and spiritual life. She fulfils all divine aspirations and grants ultimate wisdom, success, integrity and sustenance to those who appeal to her," said grandma.

When we entered the temple, I was astonished to see the beautiful decoration of goddess statue. I could sense the positive energy charge within me. As I was gifted with purple attire that day, I knew that my mother would share the attributes of purple colour that day.

When I returned home, I noticed a small parcel near the dressing table in my bedroom. There was a handwritten note, "Do you have PURPLE colour traits? It's time to explore within you. Act now." I opened the present and it was a lovely purple crystal which had the inscription - ***"Creative, Grandeur and Wisdom"***.

I immediately picked up my phone and messaged, "Mom, Thank you." I received an audio message from her as it was already 9 p.m. I tapped on the message.

PURPLE is the colour of CREATIVITY and SPIRITUALITY. This colour possesses the energy level of red with reliability of blue, making a perfect balance representing spirituality, wisdom, luxury, loyalty and courage. Purple is a magical colour that is associated with self-realization, dignity, independence, nobility and creativity. It sparks the imagination and creates new innovative ideas to solve problems.

Knowing yourself is the beginning of all wisdom.
- Aristotle

Generally, these women are courageous, intelligent, creative, imaginative and ambitious in nature. These women carry 'anything is possible' attitude. Purple is known for dignity, luxury, wisdom, royalty and power.

CREATIVE people are highly independent and bold risk takers who follow the *'Think big'* philosophy. They always carry superior attitude and big dreams that allow them to think out-of-the-box. By nature, they are CURIOUS deep thinkers, which make them successful problem solvers. These intellectual women have the ability to think of unique ways to address a problem or to improvise on the existing solutions. They are BRAVE enough to travel and thrive in the unknown and unexplored spaces.

Mallika Srinivasan is the Chairperson and CEO of Tractors and Farm Equipment Limited (TAFE), a mass manufacturer of tractors. TAFE is the third largest tractor manufacturer in the world with more than 80 branches across many countries. She is on the board of AGCO Corporation (Agricultural Equipment manufacturer), Tata Steel Limited and Tata Global Beverages Limited.

She was born in Tirunelveli, Tamil Nadu. She earned her master's degree in Econometrics from the University of Madras where she was University gold-medallist. She holds MBA from University of Pennsylvania. She also received Honorary Doctorate in Science from Tamil Nadu Agricultural University and Honorary Doctorate of Letters from Hindustan University of Technology and Science, Chennai.

She is known for her entrepreneurship and leadership skills. Within three decades, TAFE has established itself as a robust organization. Under her leadership, the company became a high technology-oriented company and became one of the most profitable tractor companies in the world. In spite of ups and downs of the company, she proved to be a determined and strong leader capable of bringing the company onto the success track. She is also a member of the governing board of both the Indian School of Business, Hyderabad, and the Rural Technology and Business Incubator at the Indian Institute of Technology, Chennai.

She has been instrumental in supporting various healthcare organizations such as Sankara Nethralaya and Cancer Hospital in Chennai. She has also contributed towards establishing several educational and healthcare facilities in her home town.

She was ranked as one of *the top 125 most successful alumni* of University of Pennsylvania. She has received numerous awards including the *Entrepreneur of the year* in manufacturing by Ernst & Young and Forbes Asia's list of the *Top 50 Asian Power Businesswomen*, to name a few. In 2018, she was ranked fifth among *India's Most Powerful Women* by Fortune India.

She is a creative and wise leader who has broken the stereotype of our society, by leading mechanical manufacturing segment.

Expect the best, plan for the worst, and
prepare to be surprised.
– Denis Waitley

Creative people are usually fascinating individuals with a wide range of interests. They possess incredible qualities and tend to be FEARLESS in their pursuits. They are generally open-minded to accept new ideas and different perspectives. These women are highly active, AMBITIOUS and give great importance to go an extra mile for every task they own. They prefer to work in challenging projects that excites them as they have deep interest in new learning experiences. This attitude helps them produce extra-ordinary results.

Shikha Sharma, an economist and banker who was the Managing Director and CEO of Axis bank for the period from 2009 till 2018, has spent three decades in the financial sector. She had travelled around various Indian cities as her father was an Indian army officer. She received her MBA from IIM Ahmedabad.

In 1980, soon after her business administration studies, she started her career with ICICI Bank. She was instrumental in setting up several initiatives in ICICI Securities – a joint venture between ICICI and J.P. Morgan. She also managed ICICI Prudential Life Insurance division. Under her leadership, the organization became the largest private sector life insurance company.

In 2009, she joined Axis Bank as the MD and CEO where she had to face different set of challenges of commercial banking. Within three years of her appointment, the bank's net profit grew by 20 percent and the bank's stock grew by 90 percent. In 2014, the Axis Bank Foundation, won the title of *'Outstanding Corporate Foundation'* at the Forbes India Philanthropy Awards. Her leadership has led the bank to receive many accolades, like *'Bank of the Year 2014 in India'* by The Banker Magazine, and *'Most Trusted Private Sector Bank'* by Economic Times, to name a few.

Though banking and insurance sectors are considered as a male dominated profession, she carved a special place for herself due to her exceptional leadership qualities. Disciplined life and work ethics have been the secret weapons for her success. She has received many recognition, personally as well, including *Banker of the Year* for 2014 - 15, *AIMA - JRD Tata Corporate Leadership Award* for the Year 2014, Forbes List of *Asia's 50 Power Business Women and Transformational Business Leader of the Year,* to name a few.

She is a role-model for young women who aspire to become a leader in their fervent profession.

Wisdom is not a product of schooling but of
the lifelong attempt to acquire it.
- Albert Einstein

These women are usually daydreamers and rule-breakers who prefer not to follow and get lost in the crowd. They are emotionally STRONG and work tirelessly to achieve their vision. They carry a great ZEAL and physical energy that helps them maintain long working hours with deep interest and involvement. They constantly SEEK new experiences and tend to be smart risk-takers. They are good observers and listeners which helped them to develop great ideas. These women remind me of Brain Tracy's words, *"Leaders are never satisfied; they continually strive to be better."*

These women were not only successful in pursuing their passionate career but also managing their personal commitments as a mother. They created support ecosystem both at workplace and at home to help them. Also some of organizational policies like work from home, flexible working hours, etc did support them to meet the demands of their children. But still they had to face several challenges and COMPROMISED on many things during initial stages of their children, but on a longer run, the challenging situation they overcame turned to be their strength and increased their CONFIDENCE to handle their workplace challenges.

Aruna Jayanthi is a businesswoman and Managing Director of Capgemini's Asia Pacific and Latin America business unit. She served as a CEO of Capgemini India from 2011 - 2016. She is also an executive council member of NASSCOM. She has been a Chairperson of the board of governors of National Institute of Technology, Calicut.

She holds a master's degree in Management Studies in Finance. In 2000, she joined Capgemini to setup the company's offshore capabilities in India. Under her administration, she made India an incubation hub. She established and scaled up various services like consulting, technology and outsourcing under their business portfolio. This move helped her to expand the Indian workforce to about 40,000 employees. Within a few years, she became the Global Delivery Head for the outsourcing division.

According to her, *"One has to have fire in the belly and a strong desire to succeed. Without that you don't get anywhere."* Her exceptional contribution to the growth of Indian business unit and focus to improve employee performance made her successful. She became the role model for breaking labels and for women empowerment.

She was listed third among the *Most Powerful Women* in 2012, by Fortune India, and appeared in *Most Powerful Women in Business* by Business Today for several years.

She says, *"IT is about creating business value to our customer. It's not about mere application of technology to the customer or about writing best program in the world. It's about our willingness to understand the customer problem correctly and solve it effectively."*

When it is obvious that the goals cannot be reached, don't adjust the goals, adjust the action steps.
- Confucius

These women are highly resilient, self-expressive and carry great EXCITEMENT to follow their true passion. They carry high energy levels and get engaged in their work losing track of time. These women purposely avoid doing things that makes life monotonous. They live with clear and focused mind and make time for 'mindfulness'. They also have the ability to manage discomfort and stress for a longer period. They are smart THINKERS who can connect the dots. They remind me of Steve Jobs' words, *"Creativity is just connecting things. It's the ability to connect experiences they've had and synthesize new things."*

Kanika Tekriwal is the founder and CEO of JetSetGo, a private jet and helicopter aggregation digital platform that manages, operates and flies private jets and helicopters for flight owners.

She hails from Bhopal. She received her bachelor's degree in Economics and diploma in Design. She had entrepreneurial thoughts from early childhood days. At the age of 17, she identified her passion in aviation and she started working on achieving it. She then completed her MBA from Coventry University, UK, which enhanced her entrepreneurial skills. While she was studying, she worked with aerospace resources in business development and discerned the potential market in India.

In 2011, after her return to India, at the age of 22, she was diagnosed with cancer. During the nine months of vigorous chemotherapy treatment she came up with the idea of JetSetGo. She used this tough phase of life to think and materialize her passion to be part of aviation industry. Though it was an unexpected journey, she had a firm determination to fight back and never gave up. She used her setback wisely to become a successful entrepreneur.

She started JetSetGo in 2014 primarily to cater to corporate business executives who had to cover meetings across multiple cities on same day. JetSetGo became helpful platform for emergency evacuations, medical emergencies and for tourists to access remote areas. The platform also offers management services for private aircrafts including on-the-ground services and ongoing maintenance checks. The company is referred as the 'Uber of the Skies' as it delivers ultimate pleasure to customers in private aviation industry.

She made it among the Forbes Asia's *30 Under 30*, a list of top 30 leading entrepreneurs below the age of 30. In 2015, she was one of the seven Indians on BBC's list of *100 most inspiring women*.

*It is courage, courage, courage that raises the
blood of life to crimson splendour.*
– Horace

A WISE person is good in handling rejections and failures. They are not afraid to say, *'I don't know.'* They tend to be good LISTENERS. Due to this quality, they are flexible and easily adapt to new environment and new people. They exhibit SELF-CONTROL which helps them to manage challenging situations positively. They have deeper understanding of the facts gained from their experience and they tolerate the unpleasant situations in life well. These women tend to be individualistic and have good sense of HUMOUR.

Chitra Ramakrishna was the first woman Managing Director and CEO of the National Stock Exchange(NSE). Under her leadership, NSE became world's largest exchange in cash market trades. She is a chartered accountant who started her career with the financial division at IDBI.

She was one among the hand-picked leadership team formed to enable the automated screen based trading system at NSE. She was the third woman to head a stock exchange in the Asia-Pacific region after those in Sri Lanka and China.

She has laid a strong foundation and took several key initiatives to launch various products to suit investors. She carries a great positive attitude to set a vision for the start-up and stood as the pillar to propel NSE onto its success path. She always felt that a start-up will not have too many expectations and thus can be flexible in creating a new path and travel to any heights. Her positive thought process helped her achieve her vision.

Her strong leadership skills and great understanding of the market were her weapons to bring NSE to success track. She was instrumental in making NSE, a modern stock exchange with pan India presence. She delivers lecture on 'Leadership Lessons in Institution Building' in top management schools at India.

She has been featured in the list of *Top 30 women achievers* by the Business Today group for four successive years. She was selected as the *Woman of the year* by the Forbes magazine recently and was also ranked 17th in the list of *Top global women business leaders* by Fortune magazine, USA.

---

*A person who never made a mistake
never tried anything new.*
– Albert Einstein

These creative and intelligent women never had any fear of going wrong. Even during tough situations, they used their failures as a learning opportunity and continued to EXPLORE alternate opportunities to achieve their vision. These women strongly believed in Bertrand Russell's words, *"To conquer fear is the beginning of wisdom."* They always had the CURIOSITY of a child to learn new things. This helped them improve on out-of-box thinking styles to solve complex problems.

On this ninth night of Navaratri, I want you to think about these qualities to become a vibrant woman. Lead a SELF-DISCIPLINED life with self-control. You need to learn how to PRIORITIZE to meet all your commitments at home and work. Be open-minded and make learning a continuous activity throughout your life. Be a bold risk-taker by knowing how to take calculated risks. You need to learn to handle rejections and failures by taking action instead of worrying about them. I want you to incubate PURPLE colour qualities within yourself. Be creative, develop wisdom, and live an extra-ordinary life with grandeur, not only uplifting your family but also the society.

*To live a creative life, we must lose our
fear of being wrong.*
- Joseph Chilton Pearce

The audio stopped.

That day, I learned the real success secrets of wise women. I appreciated the dedication and determination they showed to achieve their goals. I became clear that their attitude towards problems made them the role-models for youngsters of India. I admired the transformation in my thoughts after hearing mom's views in the last nine nights.

The next morning, I woke up as a completely different person and decided to live my life in a best possible way and to contribute to the society to improve the lives of a common man. I was confident that I will soon become the world's renowned scientist and bring in value to the society which will impact at least a billion lives.

I got so excited to meet my parents and my brother, Ajay. They pleasantly surprised me by visiting our home town for the weekend.

That day, my grandmother made arrangements for the final tenth day pooja, a closing ceremony, that follows the celebration of nine nights of Navaratri. Along with Ajay, Meena and grandfather, I visited our farms and had great time watching how sugarcanes are processed to produce sugar and jaggery. We all had a great evening and enjoyed exquisite dinner after the final pooja.

Chapter 11

Situational Self-Leadership

" I am the master of my fate, I am the captain of my soul. "

- **William Ernest Henley**

After a pleasant joyful day with my parents, that night, mom said to me, "Today, the tenth day, following the nine nights of Navaratri is celebrated as the day of victory of light over darkness. Let your life journey continue in bright multi-colours to lead a meaningful and fulfilling life."

Looking at the nine crystals that glittered at our bedroom study table, I questioned, "Mom, you taught me the importance of different traits that are required for a modern woman, correlating them with the nine avatars of Durga and referencing the colours which most signify those qualities. But, which is the most important trait or colour among these which I need to inculcate within me?"

"Listen Anila, all the traits or colours that I discussed with you are equally important for a modern woman. Think about how different avatars of goddess Durga had different traits, but they still correspond to the same woman, goddess Durga. Each avatar is nothing but goddess Durga's manifestation to handle a specific type of a problem / situation. Similarly every one of us should continuously strive hard to improve ourselves on all the traits. We need to learn to be SMART to employ specific traits depending on the SITUATION, in order to lead a successful and significant life filled with authentic happiness," said my mother.

I asked, "Mom, are you talking about taking control over ourselves to handle a challenging situation?"

"Yes exactly! You need to take the complete responsibility to solve a challenging situation without expecting others to solve it for you. Understand everything starts with mastering SELF.

I want to introduce you to my recommendations on 'Situational Self-Leadership.' There are two things that you need to understand here - Self-leadership and Situational leadership.

Self-leadership is all about developing our INNER-SELF by cultivating qualities like self-awareness, self-confidence, self-esteem, self-discipline, emotional intelligence, self-efficacy and living by a vision by realizing our passion and potential. You need to learn how to orient yourself in order to become a better person. You need to lead yourself to achieve your goals and to effectively lead your life by taking effective actions.

If you want to lead yourself, you should clearly know *'Who you are?'* and *'What you want to achieve in life?'* By being accountable for your actions and regulating your emotions before reacting, you can bring compelling changes to your life.

An important aspect of self-leadership is how we perceive and deal with problems. You need to cultivate a MINDSET to accept the reality and create willingness to solve the problem even before attempting to do so. The hope and positive attitude towards problem solving is the most important factor in successfully solving any complex issue.

Self-leadership is the practice of intentionally influencing your thinking, feeling and actions towards your objectives.
- Bryant and Kazan

In general, situational leadership refers to ADAPTIVE leadership style, where the leader must consider underlying circumstances before adapting the best leadership style to meet the goals of the team. In reference to self-leadership, I am talking about self and how women need to exhibit the right trait based on their interpretation of the circumstances. The self-leadership style driven by the situation is called situational self-leadership.

Remember, there is no universal quick fix. Instead, you need to learn to look at each threat with different perspectives and accordingly be flexible to exhibit the right set of qualities to handle your situation. The situation led self-leadership demands you to become a powerful woman with self-awareness, social-awareness, self-confidence, trust, positive attitude and the ability to learn with open-mind.

Effective leaders need to be flexible, and must adapt themselves according to the situation.
- Paul Hersey and Kenneth Blanchard

When I asked you to learn the trait of being calm and polite that doesn't mean that you shouldn't become assertive and controlling in in a tough challenging confrontation. You need to understand the value of both types of traits and you need to smartly CHOOSE the right one in right situation", said my mother.

I asked, "Mom, situational self-leadership is all about exploring ourselves. Is this right?"

"Anila, self-awareness is the starting point. The basic foundational step is exploring oneself and investing in self. Having a personal time for ourselves in our daily schedule would become an eye-opener to understand our life purpose. Spending at least an hour on YOURSELF – thinking about your passion, who you are, personal interests, values, ambitions, strengths, weaknesses, how you want to live your life, etc – will set a direction for you. Unless you have good clarity on the direction, you can't drive your car of life.

This personal time will help you enrich your POSITIVE thinking style. Your belief and attitude is more important than being intelligent. The game-changer personalities succeeded in their vision not because they were highly intelligent, but they believed in themselves. You become what YOU think. So, take time to observe your thoughts and build your self-esteem and self-confidence. Realize you are stronger than what you believe. This will automatically help you to get rid of your fear. Understand, YOU are more important for you than anyone else.

Learn to calm down the winds of your mind,
and you will enjoy great inner-peace.
*- **Remez Sasson***

On a busy day at my office cafeteria, I met my ex-colleague and friend, Shilpa, after a decade. She looked more energetic and younger than earlier when we had worked together. Though we were good friends then, we had lost touch in the last few years.

We quickly got re-introduced and after speaking for a while, I was sorry to know that she had divorced her husband sometime ago, as he tortured her to quit her job. As theirs was a love marriage, she didn't get much support from her parents, even after their separation. But to my surprise, instead of sharing concerns of being a single parent, she talked to me about her career achievements. She showed me her daughter's recent birthday party photos, their vacation pictures in Singapore, etc. I was still curious to understand the transformation in her, so I managed to schedule another meeting for that evening. I wanted to know the secret behind her happiness.

I cancelled all other commitments and met her that evening. I learnt how her married life turned into a tragedy. After years of abuse she finally developed courage to get rid of all bad things surrounding her. Once the thought took shape in her mind, her life transformed. She reclaimed her pride, salvaged her self-esteem and obtained a confident outlook. That day, I understood, her joyful life was her choice.

Without being sentimental, she rationally thought through various dimensions of her problem. She was able to get out of a toxic relationship and managed to legally settle down, peacefully, with her only daughter. She said, "I became stronger when my daughter got discharged from hospital after a major successful surgery." At the end of the meeting when I hugged her goodbye, a drop of my tear fell on her shoulder. She said, "Don't worry, I am doing great now. I was reborn when I decided to live my best life."

That day, I realized, how we REACT to our tough life situations decides the rest of our life. We don't have control over life circumstances but we do have good control on how we react to those events.

Being challenged in life is inevitable,
being defeated is optional.
- Roger Crawford

Paulami Patel, at the age of twelve, was terribly electrocuted, which left her with about 75 percent burns and amputated arms. 11,000 volts electric current had travelled through her right hand and left through her left foot. Her right hand was severely damaged and her left foot had no skin, muscles or tissues left. Her parents became the pillars of support in her life. After 45 surgeries, Paulami completed her MBA and currently runs her family business, which deals with heavy machinery.

She said, *"I never thought that I would face an accident and little did I know that it was going to change my life forever. But as it happened, there was nothing anyone could do to undo it. But what I could do was fight back. There were two choices—either give up and drown myself in self-pity or make peace with the situation and face it with a smile. I started seeing everything as an opportunity rather than as a hindrance. And that's what made the difference! Don't shut yourself down, don't hold back. There is so much more to life and a whole world left to conquer. When life presents you with an opportunity; grab it with both the hands. I did the same, just with 1 and a half!"*

What happens is not as important as how you react to what happens.
– Ellen Glasgow

Problems are common. But how we REACT during tough situation decides our life. Paulami is one of the best examples for Situational Self-leadership. Sometimes, our life might uncover unexpected circumstances, but we need to develop courage to face life and become an example to inspire others. She reminds me of Oprah Winfrey's words, *"Turn your wounds into wisdom."*

Dr. Umesh and **Dr. Ashwini Sawarkar** pledged to donate their three-month-daughter's organs. When their driver stepped off the vehicle to open the gates at their home, a speeding car hit their vehicle, severely injuring baby Meera and Ashwini who were in the backseat.

Baby Meera suffered severe brain injury and her survival chance was low. Ashwini, who was suffering with pelvic fracture, first uttered the words, 'organ donation.' The couple had to approach Health Ministry as the hospital declined infant organ donation. After the first confirmatory test declared Meera brain dead, two potential recipients were identified. However, before the second test to confirm the results could be done in the next 24 hours (norm in case of kids less than a year old), her heart gave away. Before Meera could save lives of two other babies she suffered cardiac arrest.

The couple said, *"Life is indeed difficult for those who are left behind to cope up with loss of their loved ones. When the doctors declared our daughter brain dead, there wasn't anything left for us to do. But together, we nursed this vision of donating our baby's organs. We believed that through organ donation, we would be able to keep the memories of our daughter alive by giving someone in need a second chance of life. It was what kept us strong through this excruciatingly painful time. More than the sadness of losing our child, what saddened us further was that this dream of ours couldn't be fulfilled. If the authorities were aware of the process or if the guidelines were in place for infant organ donation, this could have happened"*.

Whether you think you can or think you can't, you're right.
- Henry Ford

Madhu Singhal, a social activist born in Haryana with permanent visual disability, pursued her B.A and was selected as *'The Best All Rounder Student'*. She lost her father but not her hope. She relocated to Bengaluru and started 'Mithra Jyothi' in 1990 with support from her brother-in-law and her friends. This non-profit organization aims to assist people with disabilities to become independent, by providing educational support.

The charitable trust conducts various programs including computer aided training, independent life skills coaching, Braille transcription centre, job placement services and residential course for visually impaired women. Their talking book library has more than 4000 cassettes on variety of subjects. They have placed more than 600 visually impaired candidates in various jobs.

She says, *"I think God has sent everybody here for a purpose. I think every woman has a huge potential within her to achieve greater heights... The challenges women face in business are nothing but hidden opportunities for you to rise. Just go out and explore your dreams with confidence..."*

---

*Everything comes to us that belongs to us if
we create the capacity to receive it.*
– Rabindranath Tagore

In 2020, at the crucial time of Corona outbreak in India, virologist **Minal Dakhave Bhosale** delivered India's first testing kit for Covid-19 in a record time of 6 weeks. She did this just a day before delivering her daughter. This testing kit reduced the testing time from 8 to 2.5 hours that enabled the healthcare institutions to carry out their tests quickly.

Minal is the research chief of Mylab Discovery Solutions in Pune, which is the first Indian firm to get approval for making Corona virus testing kit. She says, "As *it was an emergency, I took it as a challenge to get this delivered quickly. I am happy that I could do something to serve my nation.*"

More than having the responsibility of mother-to-be, her passion towards work and patriotic thoughts helped her develop courage to successfully achieve her goal – deliver both the testing kit and her daughter. She serves as a good example for situational self-leadership.

*Victory is always possible for the person
who refuses to stop fighting.*
- Napoleon Hill

In my first organization, two of my supervisors taught me a life lesson. My former manager advised me to work hard and always pushed me to go an extra mile in every task I did. Whenever I was struck and got slowed down, he used to join me and reenergize to accomplish the task. This attitude made our team members help each other and accomplish the goal as one. During the 5 years that I worked under him, he helped me accomplish many of my career goals. And also our 10 member team won the *Best Team* award, five years in a row.

Later, when I moved to a different team, I reported to a different manager who always enjoyed delegating his work. He advised me on how to get the work done smartly from others. But as a team we were upset as we never got the credit for the work during the senior management meetings. For him, his promotion and salary hike was the only priority. This led to spread of negative energy across the team. Though each team member was good individual contributor, we were all a bit worried about who will get the credit. The insecurities that resulted led people to work on proving who was better. We as a team failed in all the project deliverables and this lead to the product failure.

Give importance to the people and environment around you. Your aspirations, traits and goals get nourished by them. Surround yourself with people who carry POSITIVITY and winning attitude. Don't let negative energy creators spoil your goals instead try your best to come out of such environment. Don't hesitate to change your team or organization, if needed.

At the same time, be friendly and kind to people around you. Don't be egoistic and always carry ready to help attitude. Only this attitude will attract good people towards you. Understand human beings have difference of opinion and we have limitations. So, don't expect everyone to be a perfectionist. Look for opportunity to SOCIALIZE with people to learn from their experiences and appreciate others for their good will and accomplishments. This will help you move along with right set of positive people.

Everything in your life is a reflection of a
choice you have made. If you want a different
result, make a different choice.
- Unknown Author

YOU are deciding how to live **YOUR** life. YOU are CHOOSING your life," concluded my mother.

I asked, "Mom, how do I continuously improve on the traits that you have detailed?"

"Your awareness on these colour traits is the first step towards acquiring them. As part of your daily morning routines, include additional 30 minutes of meditation to visualize these colour traits. All you need to do is sit down with your eyes closed and think about the traits represented by a colour and visualize as though you are exhibiting the traits in your daily activities and intensify your visual thoughts in your mind.

You don't need to cover all the colours on every day. Rather, you can practice meditating on each colour traits for 3 consecutive days in a month. This will help you to complete all the 9 colour traits within every month. This way, you could cover your awareness on all the colour traits every month and visualize them frequently," my mom completed.

I asked, "Mom, do you mean, we can acquire all these traits just by doing meditation?"

"No, Anila. I am just giving you the starting point . You need to be whole-heartedly aware that these traits are very important in your life. As you think about these traits regularly, it gets embedded in your sub-conscious mind. What you focus on consistently is what you get in your life.

The sub-conscious mind will use these traits to implement positive patterns in your life. This will involuntarily help you in tough situations to exhibit the right trait. The rest is all about what you practically learn from real life experiences, as you practice exhibiting these traits. Be a curious life-long learner," concluded my mother.

I slept with the thoughts about the need to discover and foster situation led self-leadership.

Chapter 12

The Advent of Justice

" There is a higher court than courts of justice and that is the court of conscience. It supersedes all other courts. "

- Mahatma Gandhi

I was shocked and upset after hearing the morning news. I couldn't accept the improper punishment given to Nirbhaya rape culprits. A few years of imprisonment is not what they deserve for their behaviour towards a woman. And one of the accused, being a minor, was send to a reform facility for three years. I was lost in thoughts, wondering if a minor wasn't behaving like one while committing a crime, why should he be considered so while administering a punishment.

I was horrified when my mother shared the findings of Madhumita Pandey, a 27-year-old student researcher. She interviewed convicted rapists in Tihar jail for her doctoral thesis in Criminology from Anglia Ruskin University in Cambridge, UK. Her interviews confirmed that in general, rapists had a poor opinion about women and they presented themselves as non-repentant and attempted to justify their crimes.

The report states, *"In the sample of 100 convicted rapists, most were uneducated and from rural backgrounds however this in no way suggests that rapes are only committed by uneducated men from struggling socio-economic backgrounds. Urbanization does bring exposure which can be useful in altering traditional mindsets and education of course plays a vital role in creating awareness to reduce such crimes. Not all men convicted of rape took responsibility for their crimes or expressed a sense of remorse. Most men did not identify their actions as wrong and they did not feel like they had anything to apologise for."*

This report clearly indicates that these culprits aren't feeling guilty or remorseful of their crime. One could argue that knowledge and illiteracy plays a monstrous role and hence educating men should help addressing this issue. However, I strongly feel that this will have painfully slow and limited effect. Instead tightening the law – punishing the culprits severely – would automatically create both the awareness and act as warning; Thus creating safer environment for women more swiftly.

Effective parenting, teenage education, and women safety and public awareness initiatives, among others would act as a preventive measure in reducing such issues in future. Education on morality is the most agreeable option. When the situation turns worse, our judicial system should dissuade the public by convicting the criminals with stringent revolutionary punishments, serving as the next best option to reduce crimes against women. In a way, harsh punishment would also serve as the best defence and to educate men on the need for women's safety.

Though India has seen many thriving women leaders and game-changers across various business domains, unfortunately, we are still fighting for love, care and safer environment well deserved by every Indian woman, even after 73 years of Independence.

Our ancient Indian monarchy was better. At least, the accused were immediately punished and sometimes publicly executed. This terrified others who would have a thought of committing such crimes in future. May be this helped the king to easily maintain law and order better than our current Indian judicial system.

Unfortunately, our court cases filed 15 to 20 years back are still waiting for judgement. This lag and gaps in our judicial system is the biggest advantage for the criminals to continue their offenses. Though fast-track courts were introduced to deal with rape cases, limitations in judicial resources has led to backlogs of thousands of cases. India has a ratio of 14 judges per million people – among the lowest in United Nation study of 65 nations. Besides this, there are many organizations that come forward to accept curative petition to release the culprits from their original sentencing as an act of courtesy.

In a developing country like India, judicial system plays the most important role in maintaining the rights of people, law and order – including women safety. Considering the attitude of convicted rapists, is it not important for the government to bring key initiatives for educating men and to tighten the law to create fear among the men who would think of such acts in future? When will Indian women get justice? Who will come forward to help us?

Since, I neither have the authority nor I am a law graduate to dive deep and recommend refinement of our laws, I decided to take some steps for my personal satisfaction.

After spending twelve memorable days at our home town, we – my parents, Ajay and me – bid adieu to my grandparents and got into the car. We headed towards Bengaluru. Words cannot explain the value of the learning and inspiration that I have received, in the last twelve days, to face life as it unfolds.

After a lot of analysis and support from my mother, we decided to create two teams – RED Team and BLUE Team that would independently operate to fulfil two different objectives. We wanted RED team to investigate the sexual violence crimes and identify the gaps in our judicial system. We wanted BLUE team to work on educational and rehabilitation support for victims of these crimes. We created a charter with – the objectives, priority list of activities and expected outcome – for both the teams.

RED Team

The six-month charter had two phases of equal duration. I kick started the phase I activities immediately after reaching Bengaluru. Using the power of social media, I connected with my school alumni and other friends to get their support. I listed down the girls who appeared for Indian civil services examination – Union Public Services Commission (UPSC) and those who graduated from Army school in the last few years. I was able to garner the names and information of 15 girls. I had a detailed discussion to understand their career aspiration in life.

My mother analysed various factors including their family situation, maturity level, age, financial commitments, social interest, etc and created the acceptance criteria for selection into our team. Another important yardstick we had was that they should have had at least 2 failed attempts in UPSC exam. This helped us select like-minded and highly motivated people with social awareness attitude.

We finally handpicked only 9 out of these 15 girls, to be part of our plan. We went in person and met each of these 9 girls multiple times to discuss our objectives without revealing the details of our Team Red plans. After 3 months, we shortlisted 6 girls who were actually ready for the game.

Now that we had a 6 member team, knowledgeable of the civil service field, we commenced Phase II. We, as a team, researched and identified 15 women who could help us in executing our RED Team mission. We met all these 15 women and discussed in detail about their interest in social service, perspectives on social responsibility, etc. We had to drop-out a few women in the middle due to various reasons and finally, we were able to double our team.

The like-minded 12 members, agreed to align themselves with RED team without expecting any salary. They were inducted with the oath – "We will secretly work for the next 10 years and keep this a secret mission." To avoid any doubts from family and society, the 12 member women team took up jobs as journalists in their respective cities.

Since the average age of the women in this team was about 25 years, these women promised not to take up any other job and agreed to spend the next 10 years for the benefit of the society.

In the next 6 months, the focused group of 12 women started functioning in Tamil Nadu, Kerala and Karnataka, by forming a four-member team in each state. The teams worked on a common objective – investigate and collect the required proofs about any sexual violence crimes against women in the respective states.

The team RED was made very clear on their strategies and work ethics. They knew that they were not supposed to take law in their hands. They were clearly instructed about the expectations from them. They were trained to handle the investigations strategically so that their reports might compliment police investigations in future.

This team targeted to secretly investigate any sexual harassment crimes against women by speaking to the victims in person and collecting possible proofs about the culprit. The team also investigated whether or not legal punishments were apportioned to the criminals.

The submitted proofs were carefully analysed and assessed by the peer members of the team and finally, a copy of the proof was shared with their chief trainer, a retired female Supreme Court judge. She readily agreed to support us for this cause and became the backbone of Team Red, in strategizing the activities according to the team's vision. Her coaching on managing Intelligence

Quotient (IQ) and Emotional Quotient (EQ) helped the team to effectively accomplish their tasks.

BLUE Team

Through the social connections of my mother and her friends, we met many social activists across various Indian states. We identified a team of 15 retired women who were army officers, social workers, lawyers, gymnasts, police officers, teachers, doctors, college principals, athletes and physiotherapists. We explained the objectives of BLUE Team, and they unanimously agreed to work together – to support women victims of sexual violence crimes. The average age of this like-minded team was about 60 years.

This team was headed by a retired female IAS officer. As planned, the BLUE Team registered a non-profit organization – *W-Cross foundation,* which would provide medical, psychological and legal support to women who were undergoing mental trauma resulting from sexual harassment.

This foundation would not only provide counselling to women victims and train them on various life skills including self-defence, independence, women's rights awareness, communication and education but also provides educational programs and awareness workshops to prevent such crimes. The foundation would also help in providing job opportunities, based on individual's educational qualifications.

It took more than a year for the W-cross team to establish a centre and to spread its wings to partner with various NGOs including Majlis Manch, Prajwala, Azad foundation, Guria, One Stop Crisis Centre, ActionAid association, Lawyers Collective, Angala and Prerana. The team also conducted workshops and seminars in schools, colleges and public places to create awareness on the importance of sexual education.

Several sexual education methodologies were published to bring awareness from kindergarten to college grads. With the help of both male and female volunteers from public, the foundation expanded the training programs to provide innovative public awareness workshops. A dedicated educational track led by men was created to emphasize on the sex education for men. This track helped to impart moral values about gender-equality and women empowerment among men.

Deliberately, the team Blue W-cross foundation members weren't made aware of the existence of team Red; Though team Red indirectly referred many women victims to team Blue for support through W-cross foundation, both teams were purposely isolated.

At the end of first year, as the team Red and team Blue started functioning, we rolled out the roadmap for the next two years. Based on the crime rate, we identified the top districts within each state and started monitoring them.

Team Red moved in into the respective districts and was on its toes to execute its tasks. The member's identity as a journalist / press, helped them easily connect with the locals and get the support. They collected every possible lead and clues about crimes against women even before the rest of the media. The most heartening thing was that they personally met the victims and were thus able to provide them with courage and routed them to team Blue to undergo formal counselling and for legal guidance.

RED Team Expansion

In the next two years, team Red reported more than 120 cases – with detailed information about the cases along with investigation records. The most shocking data was 80 percent of the criminals weren't tracked by law, as they managed to escape using false proofs or sentenced to few years of imprisonment only. This helped the team leader, the retired Supreme Court judge, to bring these reports directly to Prime Minister's notice using her powerful connections.

Their reports not only highlighted the decrease in the conviction rates for rapists but also outlined the gaps in the current judicial system. The report quantitatively highlighted those men who escaped conviction and the officials who supported these criminals to escape from conviction.

Team Red couldn't believe that the Prime Minister(PM) had invited them for a secret personal meeting. Their meeting with PM was fruitful and their impressive work, risking their personal lives, finally created value for the nation. As per PM's order, the team's investigation reports served as a good foundation for the senior counsel of lawyers to relook at the women safety laws and analyse the major gaps in it.

The team head also shared a copy of all their reports with the top 5 social media channel CEOs, without sharing their personal identity, and with a warning to disclose the data to public only if the criminals were not legally punished within 6 months of report submission. This added pressure to convict all the rapists of the reported cases.

Prime Minister approved Team Red's requisitions and recommended legal departments to revisit the laws to bring amendments to it. As the authorities who supported the criminals were permanently dismissed from their jobs without any provision for plea, this created huge pressure among the officials to strictly adhere to the new policy changes.

The newly created central government team assisted team Red to continue their mission and promised to help with required background support to expand their operation. Additional team recruits were added after careful personal assessment. This helped the 12 member women team to spread their wings and operate In 7 additional states which had the highest reported rape cases in

India – Mizoram, Tripura, Assam, Madhya Pradesh, Haryana, Chhattisgarh and Delhi - to carry out their investigation activities secretly.

With the help of 50 member team, these women successfully investigated sexual violence crimes against women and reported more than 15,000 cases in the new states within next five years. Every quarter, they reported the crimes and ensured that the criminals were strictly punished for their behaviour – either executed immediately in front of public and in few cases, rapists were chemically castrated.

BLUE Team Expansion

Most sexual violence crimes go unreported because the victims fear humiliation. The National Crime Records Bureau (NCRB) of India 2016 report stated, "…about 71% of the rape crimes go unreported." Despite that, NCRB report 2018 stated, "…the number of rape cases doubled since 2001" - with a shocking statistics of 1 rape every 15 minutes in India.

Team Blue brought in several new initiatives to make women break their silence and speak out, like #MeToo. W-Cross created a 'safe-place' and provided supportive ecosystem that allowed many women to courageously report sexual assaults, even those that took place several years ago. The organization opened up new online reporting options to enable women to speak about their sexual harassment incidents anonymously. The platform provided legal and financial support to women to take their case to special courts for justice.

Many International women's organizations supported W-Cross. At the end of their five year plan, team Blue reported 26,000 women victims who were counselled at their centre. The foundation raised funds through governmental support and expanded to a 5000 member volunteer team with centres in all states of India. The foundation brought in several initiatives to safeguard women against violence that received huge appreciation across countries around the world.

Closure of Ten Year Plan

Every year, in the annual general body review meeting with PM, team Red highlighted the challenges they experienced during their investigation. This helped PM to emphasize the government authorities to revisit the judicial laws to close the gaps. This also helped government to consistently bring in new initiatives every year to improve the women's safety measures.

During the tenth year of their mission, a special women court was instituted to primarily deal with sexual violence cases against women. To support this court, 10 dedicated women IPS officers were appointed in every state who would investigate sexual violence crimes independently and work towards reducing them. This special court directly reports to Supreme Court senior counsel and doesn't interfere with the district level women's courts, which is operational across all Indian states. The judgements provided by this special court are personally reported to Prime Minister.

Several new amendments were made to Indian Penal Code (IPC) sections 354 and 376, to increase the severity of the punishment passed to the culprits – death sentence irrespective of age or status within 3 months or chemical castration. The accused proved of their guilt would be hanged in public place or castrated. These strict changes in the punishment created a huge impact among the public to understand the importance given by our country towards women safety.

Though many consider castration punishment, to be in direct violation of Article 21 of the Indian Constitution, "Right to Life", it was suggested by Delhi sessions judge in 2011. In 2015, Madras High Court suggested central government to consider castration as the punishment for brutal rape of toddlers. Though there were several complaints against castration but finally it was incorporated under IPC.

As requested by the Red team members, their identities were never disclosed to public though they did an extra-ordinary work spending ten years to improve women's safety measures. Their work brought in huge improvement in our judicial laws that helped to reduce the sexual crimes against women.

At the completion of their ten year stint, some of the Red team members moved out to meet with their personal commitments, though a few continued, taking charge in various positions in the nation-wide movement setup by Indian government.

Team Blue expanded its W-cross centres across India to every state with about 130 regional centres throughout the country.

In the span of 10 years, India took charge of the situation and brought in several safety measures to make India, the safest place for women and children. The Georgetown University's Institute for Women, Peace and Security (GIWPS) releases its annual report on Women, Peace, and Security Index. The report uses 11 sub-indicators to rank which country is best for women. The 2019 report ranked India at 133 out of 167 countries whereas in the year 2030, GIWPS annual report ranked India at #1.

I reminded Lois McMaster Bujold's words, *"The dead cannot cry out for justice. It is a duty of the living to do so for them."* I felt proud of India and wanted to shout out loud, "It's our tribute to you, Nirbhaya. REST IN PEACE!"

I slowly opened my eyes as mom woke me up. I realized that we had just reached Bengaluru. With a strong belief that my dream will come true soon, I stepped out of the car positively to work hard to transform my dream into a reality.

I walked into our home with the answer to my earlier questions –
*"When will Indian women get justice? Who will come forward to
help us?"*

---

*We are what our thoughts have made us; So
take care about what you think.
Words are secondary. Thoughts live; they
travel far.*
– Swami Vivekananda

Note: Nirbhaya (means 'fearless') gang rape and murder happened
in Delhi on 16th Dec 2012. After 7 years, the culprits - Akshay
Thakur, Pawan Gupta, Vinay Sharma, and Mukesh Singh were
hanged in Tihar jail on 20th March 2020. There was also a minor
involved in this crime, who was given 3 years imprisonment in a
reform centre, and has been released after serving his term.
However, in keeping with the law, juvenile rapist's identity was
never revealed.

Women Personalities Index

Night 1 (Orange Colour) : Enthusiasm, Socialism and Success

    I. Deepa Malik (Paralympics Sports Champion)
   II. Pranjal Patil (IAS Officer)
  III. Bani Yadha (Motorsports Rally Champion)
  IV. Indra Nooyi (ex-CEO, PepsiCo)
   V. Arunima Sinha (Mountaineer)

Night 2 (White Colour) : Simplicity, Calmness and Inner-Peace

    I. Sudha Murthy (Founder, Infosys Foundation)
   II. Mother Teresa (Founder, Missionaries of Charity)
  III. Lata Mangeshkar (Playback Singer)
  IV. Shaheen Mistri (CEO, Teach for India)
   V. Indu Jain (ex-CEO, Times Group)

Night 3 (Red Colour) : Passion, Strength and Courage

    I. Laxmi Agarwal (Founder, Chhanv Foundation)
   II. Avani Chaturvedi (First Indian Women Fighter Pilot of IAF)
  III. Nusrat Khan Pahade (Founder, Cactus Foundation)
  IV. Kriti Bharti (Founder, Saarthi Trust)
   V. Rani Rampal (Indian Women's Hockey Team Captain)

Night 4 (Blue Colour) : Responsible, Reliable and Honest

    I. Indu Malhotra (Supreme Court Judge)
   II. Tessy Thomas (Director General, DRDO)
  III. Kamala Selvaraj (Gynaecologist, Infertility Treatment Pioneer)
  IV. Kiran Bedi (Retired IPS Officer, Social Activist)
   V. Kalpana Chawla (Late Astronaut)

Night 5 (Yellow Colour) : Warmth, Happiness and Optimism

    I.   Bhakti Sharma (Open Water Swimmer)
   II.   P.T.Usha (Retired Athlete, Sports Champion)
  III.   Aditi Pant (Oceanographer)
  IV.   Sathyasri Sharmila (First Indian Transgender Lawyer)
   V.   Saina Nehwal (Badminton Champion)

Night 6 (Green Colour) : Growth, Health and Harmony

    I.   Sunita Narain (Environmentalist)
   II.   Mary Kom (Boxing Champion)
  III.   Harshwanti Bisht (Mountaineer, Himalaya Saver)
  IV.   Saikhom Mirabai Chanu (Weight-lifting Champion)
   V.   Preetha Reddy (Vice Chairperson, Apollo Hospitals)

Night 7 (Grey Colour) : Authority, Maturity and Neutrality

    I.   Gita Gopinath (Economist)
   II.   Nirupama Rao (Retired Foreign Secretary and Ambassador)
  III.   Ritu Kapur (CEO, Quintillion Media)
  IV.   Naina Lal Kidwai (ex-CEO, HSBC Bank)
   V.   Kiran Mazumdar (Chairperson, Biocon)

Night 8 (Pink Colour) : Care, Compassion and Hope

    I.   Aparna Lavakumar (Police officer)
   II.   Kousalaya Periysamy (Founder, Positive Women's Network)
  III.   Manasi Pradhan (Founder, Nirbhaya Vahini)
  IV.   Sunitha Krishnan (Founder, Prajwala)
   V.   Lakshmi Menon (Founder, Pure Living)

Night 9 (Purple Colour) : Creative, Grandeur and Wisdom

I.   Mallika Srinivasan (Chairperson, TAFE)
II.   Shikha Sharma (CEO, AXIS Bank)
III.   Aruna Jyanthi (ex-CEO, Capgemini)
IV.   Kanika Tekriwal (Founder, JetSetGo)
V.   Chitra Ramakrishna (ex-CEO, National Stock Exchange)

Appendix I – Know the IPC Sections

Indian Penal Code (IPC) is the official criminal code of India. As of 2018, IPC is divided into 23 chapters and contains a total of 511 sections. Various IPC sections related to offences related to affecting human body are included in **Chapter XVI: Sections 299 to 377**

Here are the IPC Sections related to sexual harassment crimes.

Section	Offence	Punishment
Section 354	Assault or use of criminal force to woman with intent to outrage her modesty	1 to 5 years and Fine
Section 354A	Sexual harassment of the nature of unwelcome physical contact and advances or a demand or request for sexual favours or showing pornography	Up to 3 years or Fine or Both
Section 354B	Criminal force to woman with intent to disrobe	3 to 7 years and Fine
Section 354C	Voyeurism	1 to 3 years and Fine for first conviction 3 to 7 years and Fine for second or subsequent conviction
Section 354D	Stalking	Up to 3 years and Fine for first conviction Up to 5 years and Fine for second or subsequent conviction
Section 372	Selling or letting to hire a minor for purposes of prostitution, etc	10 Years and Fine
Section 373	Buying or obtaining possession of a minor for the same purposes	10 Years and Fine
Section 375/376	Rape	Rigorous Imprisonment for 10 years to

		Imprisonment for Life and Fine
Section 376A	Person committing an offence of rape and inflicting injury which causes death or causes the woman to be in a persistent vegetative state	Rigorous Imprisonment for 20 years to Imprisonment for Natural-Life or Death
Section 376C	Sexual intercourse by a person in authority	Rigorous Imprisonment for 5 to 10 years and Fine
Section 376D	Gang Rape	Rigorous Imprisonment for 20 years to Imprisonment for Natural-Life and Fine paid to the victim
Section 376 AB	Person committing an offence of rape on a woman under twelve years of age	Rigorous Imprisonment for 20 years to Imprisonment for Natural-Life and Fine or Death
Section 376 DA	Gang rape on a woman under sixteen years of age	Imprisonment for Natural-Life and Fine
Section 376 DB	Gang rape on a woman under twelve years of age	Imprisonment for Natural-Life and Fine or Death
Section 377	Unnatural Offences	Imprisonment for Life or 10 Years and Fine

Appendix II – Colour Psychology References

Wikipedia says, *"Colour psychology is the study of hues as a determinant of human behaviour. Colour influences perceptions that are not obvious, such as the taste of food."* It is a well-known but less explored branch of study about how our brain perceives the colour visuals.

I would acknowledge the below online portals that helped me to study about colour psychology.

https://www.colorpsychology.org

https://www.empower-yourself-with-color-psychology.com

https://www.scienceofpeople.com/color-psychology

https://www.graf1x.com/color-psychology-emotion-meaning-poster

https://www.color-meanings.com

https://www.nickkolenda.com/color-psychology

https://www.quicksprout.com/psychology-of-color

https://www.colormatters.com/

http://www.color-wheel-pro.com/

https://www.persuasion-nation.com/blog/the-psychology-of-colors-in-marketing-how-they-influence-what-we-buy

Appendix III – Women Personalities References

I would acknowledge the below online portals that helped me to study various women leader biographies.

https://www.wikipedia.org
https://www.britannica.com
https://www.thebetterindia.com
https://www.wikibio.in
https://www.notablebiographies.com
https://www.famous-entrepreneurs.com
https://www.leaderbiography.com
https://www.kreedon.com
https://www.filmibeat.com
https://www.businessinsider.in
https://www.thefamouspeople.com
https://www.iloveindia.com
https://www.mapsofindia.com
https://www.celebrityborn.com
https://www.fortuneindia.com
https://www.buzzwhoop.com
https://www.starsunfolded.com
https://www.lifebeyondnumbers.com
https://www.yourstory.com
https://www.mbarendezvous.com

Thank You!

Thank You For Reading My Book!

I really appreciate all of your feedback, and I love hearing what you have to say.
I need your input to make the next version of this book and my future books even better.

Please leave me a helpful review on Amazon letting me know what you thought of the book.

Thank you so much!

Ramya R. Moorthy

Book link on Amazon: https://www.amazon.in/dp/8194471281

Goodreads: https://www.goodreads.com/book/show/53208955